GERMANY'S ROMANTIC ROAD
(ROMANTISCHE STRASSE)

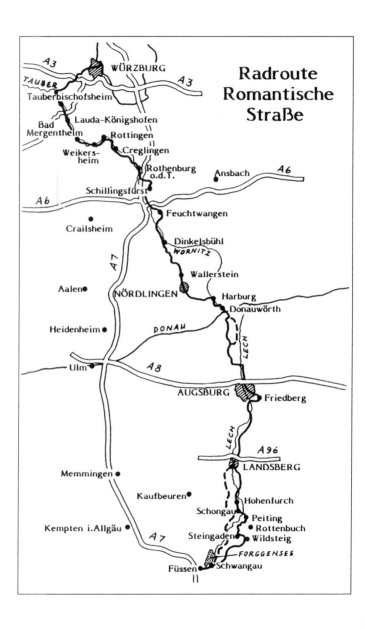

Radroute
Romantische
Straße

GERMANY'S ROMANTIC ROAD
(ROMANTISCHE STRASSE)
A Route for Cyclists and Walkers

by
Gordon McLachlan

CICERONE PRESS
MILNTHORPE, CUMBRIA

ISBN 1 85284 233 4
A catalogue record for this book is available from the British Library

ACKNOWLEDGEMENTS

The author would like to thank the staff of all the tourist offices who helped in the presentation of this book. Particular thanks are due to Ute Meesmann (Würzburg), Johannes Kempter (Rothenburg ob der Tauber), Rainer Pfahl (Bad Mergentheim), Joachim Kühne (Creglingen), Ingrid Metzner (Dinkelsbühl) and Agatha Suess of the German National Tourist Office in London.

Front Cover: The Alpsee, with a view towards Schloss Hohenschwangau

CONTENTS

Harburg, the courtyard of the Schloss (Stage 12)

INTRODUCTION

The Romantic Road or Romantische Strasse between Füssen and Würzburg is Germany's oldest tourist route. It has served as the inspiration for a host of other routes, though none of these has ever come near to matching its popularity or fame.

As its name suggests, the Romantic Road perfectly encapsulates the romanticised image of Germany as a land of quaint old walled towns, rustic villages, ornate pilgrimage churches, dramatically sited castles and splendid palaces. While this picture may stand firmly at odds with its role in 20th century history, it is nonetheless an accurate reflection of one of the faces of this most enigmatic of nations.

Not the least of the route's attractions is the way it presents such a satisfying cross-section of the southern half of Germany in all its many aspects. Along the way, a fascinating historical tapestry is unfolded. With the exception of two short sorties into Baden-Württemberg, the entire stretch of the Romantic Road lies within Bavaria (Bayern), the largest of the sixteen provinces or Länder which constitute the modern German federal state. However, the towns along its length bear witness to the centuries prior to the Napoleonic Wars, when literally hundreds of quasi-independent states dotted the map of Germany.

In this heavily decentralized framework, the Romantic Road's celebrated trio of timed-warped walled towns - Rothenburg ob der Tauber, Dinkelsbühl and Nördlingen - each functioned for centuries as city-states. The much larger city of Augsburg likewise had this status as did, albeit for much shorter periods, Donauwörth and Feuchtwangen. Though even now hardly more than villages, Harburg, Wallerstein, Schillingsfürst and Weikersheim were all proud capitals of similarly autonomous principalities, as their outsized castles testify. Würzburg was the capital of a powerful prince-bishopric while Bad Mergentheim, nowadays a plush spa, was for three centuries the headquarters of the Teutonic Knights, the premier order of German chivalry.

The Romantic Road is richly endowed with architectural and artistic treasures, many of which are of the very highest rank. In all of Europe, there are only a handful of towns with medieval fortifications to rival those of Rothenburg, Dinkelsbühl and Nördlingen, while the parish churches of these same towns, erected as symbols of municipal pride and self-confidence when they were at the height of their prosperity, are supreme examples of late Gothic. Augsburg has the grandest and most stylish Renaissance public buildings to be found anywhere north of the Alps, and this assemblage forms a fitting legacy of its period as Europe's banking capital. Among the crowning glories of the age of Baroque and Rococo are the Würzburg Residenz, which surpasses any of the continent's royal palaces in splendour, and the Wieskirche near Steingaden, which is often justifiably described as the most beautiful pilgrimage church in the world. No building better exemplifies the ideals and obsessions of 19th century Romanticism than Schloss Neuschwanstein above Hohenschwangau, a seemingly impossible fantasy turned into reality.

While the Romantic Road is primarily renowned for its cultural legacies, it also passes through many widely contrasting landscapes. These include the towering peaks of the Alpine chain of the Ammergebirge; the lush meadows, fields and woods of the pre-Alpine country known as the Pfaffenwinkel; the broad valley of the River Lech; the gentler valleys of the Wörnitz and Tauber; the vast, moon-like Ries crater; and the plateau of the Frankenhöhe. It also briefly visits the valleys of two of Germany's most important rivers, the Danube and the Main.

Until quite recently, the Romantic Road was regarded almost exclusively as a motoring route. Beginning at Füssen, this follows the B17 to Augsburg (from where a detour is necessary to reach Friedberg), then continues along the B2 to Donauwörth. There it switches to the B25, following it all the way to Rothenburg, except for a short diversion to Schillingsfürst. From Rothenburg, it proceeds via the minor roads along the side of the River Tauber to Tauberbischofsheim, from where the B27 leads to the northern terminus of Würzburg.

This makes for an excellent motoring holiday; even allowing for the time to get there from the UK and back, it can comfortably be covered in a fortnight if so desired. However, for those with more time to spare, the new Romantic Road cycling route, which is equally suitable for walkers, makes for a yet more enticing alternative.

Avoiding the main roads of the established motoring route altogether, this travels between the same 26 designated staging-posts along a mixture of specially laid paths (from which motorized transport is banned altogether), farm and forest tracks (where the odd agricultural or forestry vehicle may be encountered) and very minor roads (none of which sees much in the way of traffic).

It should be noted that, far from being the short-cut one might expect, this route is actually some 70km longer than its motoring counterpart, at times adopting a course that can best be characterized as mazy. However, the gains are considerable, adding a whole new dimension to travelling along the Romantic Road. Whereas those travelling by car tend to see little more than the setpiece tourist attractions, walkers and cyclists also experience the unspoiled countryside that lies away from the main roads, passing through dozens of villages untouched by the effects of mass tourism, where a traditional rural lifestyle - albeit one which manages to share in the general prosperity of modern Germany - is still the norm.

Although this book contains a good deal of information which can be used by those wanting to travel the Romantic Road by car, it is primarily aimed at walkers and cyclists. The first part deals with planning a trip along the route and other practicalities. In the second part, each stage of the walking and cycling route is described in turn. Detailed descriptions are given of all the designated staging-posts.

PLANNING THE TRIP

When to go

Any time from April to October inclusive should be suitable for
travelling the Romantic Road. The other months can be discounted
altogether, due to the shortness of the daylight, the likelihood of
encountering snow and other bad weather, and the fact that many
sightseeing attractions operate very reduced opening hours, or else
are closed altogether.

Germany has a temperate climate, not so different from that of
Britain, with a fairly even spread of rainfall throughout the year. As
good weather can never be guaranteed at any particular time it is
difficult to suggest any particular period as being preferable to
another. However, July and August are perhaps best avoided if at
all possible: not only are they the busiest months for tourism, they
can also be rather hotter than is ideal for long walks or cycle rides,
with the Alpine areas in particular being prone to thunderstorms.

May and June offer the advantage of long days - an important
consideration for those wanting to cover as much ground in as short
a timescale as possible. Although the countryside is beautiful in late
springtime, when the orchard trees are in blossom, it is arguably at
its most picturesque in September and (especially) October, when
it bursts into a kalaedoscopic array of autumn colours. However,
the rapidly decreasing amount of daylight during the latter month
is a distinct disadvantage.

Cycling versus walking

The Romantic Road is an ideal cycling route. Even the longest stages
can be covered comfortably in well under a day, and the almost total
absence of steep climbs makes for easy and pleasant riding. If there
is a snag, it is that the bike is of little use for exploring any of the main
towns along the way, which can only be appreciated to best
advantage on foot.

As a walking route, the Romantic Road has a couple of potential
drawbacks. By no means all the scenery measures up to that of the
Alpine and pre-Alpine stages, or of the Tauber valley, which are
splendid walks in their own right, even without taking into account
the attractions of the towns along the way. Elsewhere (notably in the
Ries and the Frankenhöhe), the route passes through a fair bit of

rather featureless farmland, and accordingly some rather monotonous walking has to be endured.

Another point to note is that the stages between Landsberg and Friedberg and between Augsburg and Donauwörth are each a demanding day's walk, the accomplishment of which could be problematic outside the months of long daylight. In both cases, there is a virtual dearth of accommodation en route, leaving public transport as the only option of last resort.

North to south versus south to north
One of the most important considerations in planning a trip along the Romantic Road is to decide whether to travel from north to south or south to north. Each is equally valid: the official waymarkings point in both directions, and there is no overriding reason to prefer one to the other.

Given the difference in altitude between Würzburg and Füssen, it might appear that the choice is between going uphill or downhill - the normal implication being that the former is for those wanting more of a challenge, the latter for those preferring a more relaxed approach. However, this distinction turns out to be almost entirely false: the gradients are so gentle that the amount of energy expended is virtually the same in either direction.

A more relevant matter is the choice of climax. Here the alternatives are nicely contrasted: either the small town of Füssen, in the shadow of the Alps and the Bavarian royal castles, or the city of Würzburg, which is as renowned for its wines and gastronomy as for its magnificent monumental heritage. Either makes a fitting end to the journey, and the choice between them can be left to personal preference.

From the scenic point of view, the main advantage in choosing to take the southbound route lies in the distant views of the Alps that appear in the later stages of the journey - though these can, of course, also be seen by looking backwards when travelling north. The northbound route, in contrast, has the very tangible advantage of following the flow of the Lech and the Tauber, the two rivers which are such prominent and recurrent features of the Romantic Road. It is largely for the last reason that it was decided to arrange this book in the form of a journey from south to north.

Distance chart

In the following chart, each of the Romantic Road's 26 official staging-posts is listed. The left-hand column shows its altitude above sea-level in metres; the right-hand columns its distance in kilometres from each of the termini. Note also that the chart follows the traditional route from Steingaden to Peiting via Wildsteig and Rottenbuch, rather than the direct course of the official cycle and walking route, which is 6km shorter. Because of the existence of alternative routes on some of the stages, it is sometimes necessary to add or subtract the odd kilometre from the figures given.

Altitude	Stage	Distance northbound	Distance southbound
808	Füssen	0	423
796	Schwangau	6	417
763	Steingaden	32	391
882	Wildsteig	39	384
763	Rottenbuch	43	380
718	Peiting	52	371
710	Schongau	56	367
699	Hohenfurch	63	360
587	Landsberg am Lech	90	333
514	Friedberg	133	290
491	Augsburg	140	283
417	Donauwörth	188	235
434	Harburg	203	220
432	Nördlingen	223	200
441	Wallerstein	227	196
441	Dinkelsbühl	262	161
455	Feuchtwangen	275	148
512	Schillingsfürst	295	128
424	Rothenburg ob der Tauber	311	112
277	Creglingen	331	92
243	Röttingen	343	80
229	Weikersheim	351	72
205	Bad Mergentheim	364	59
192	Lauda	376	47
181	Tauberbischofsheim	384	39
177	Würzburg	423	0

Suggested itineraries
Several of the 25 stages of the Romantic Road are very short, and by
no means all of them warrant a full day. The absolute minimum
amount of time needed to accomplish the entire journey, including
stops for visiting the most important sights, is two weeks for
cyclists, three weeks for walkers. Suggested itineraries for each of
these are as follows:

CYCLING
Day 1   Füssen-Schwangau
Day 2   Schwangau-Steingaden-Wildsteig-Rottenbuch-Peiting
Day 3   Peiting-Schongau-Hohenfurch-Landsberg
Day 4   Landsberg-Friedberg-Augsburg
Day 5   Augsburg
Day 6   Augsburg-Donauwörth
Day 7   Donauwörth-Harburg-Nördlingen
Day 8   Nördlingen-Wallerstein-Dinkelsbühl
Day 9   Dinkelsbühl-Feuchtwangen-Schillingsfürst-
             Rothenburg
Day 10   Rothenburg
Day 11   Rothenburg-Creglingen-Röttingen-Weikersheim
Day 12   Weikersheim-BadMergentheim-Lauda-
             Tauberbischofsheim
Day 13   Tauberbischofsheim-Würzburg
Day 14   Würzburg

WALKING
Day 1   Füssen-Schwangau
Day 2   Schwangau-Steingaden
Day 3   Steingaden-Wildsteig-Rottenbuch-Peiting
Day 4   Peiting-Schongau-Hohenfurch
Day 5   Hohenfurch-Landsberg
Day 6   Landsberg-Friedberg
Day 7   Friedberg-Augsburg
Day 8   Augsburg
Day 9   Augsburg-Donauwörth
Day 10   Donauwörth-Harburg
Day 11   Harburg-Nördlingen

Day 12	Nördlingen-Wallerstein-Dinkelsbühl
Day 13	Dinkelsbühl-Feuchtwangen
Day 14	Feuchtwangen-Schillingsfürst-Rothenburg
Day 15	Rothenburg
Day 16	Rothenburg-Creglingen
Day 17	Creglingen-Röttingen-Weikersheim
Day 18	Weikersheim-Bad Mergentheim
Day 19	Bad Mergentheim-Lauda-Tauberbischofsheim
Day 20	Tauberbischofsheim-Würzburg
Day 21	Würzburg

These itineraries should leave time for at least a cursory exploration of all the designated staging-posts along the route, particularly if travelling during the months when the daylight hours are at their longest. However, a more satisfactory and comprehensive exploration of the Romantic Road requires an extension of upwards of a week to each itinerary.

Augsburg and Würzburg both warrant a stay of two or (preferably) three days, and Rothenburg easily justifies a second day. Landsberg, Nördlingen, Dinkelsbühl and Bad Mergentheim are all well worth a full day each, while those wanting to visit the environs of the last-named, or to sample its spa facilities, will require to stay at least twice as long. Nowhere is the scope for extensions to the itinerary greater than in the magnificent Alpine scenery in the vicinity of Füssen and Schwangau, where there are enough walking trails to last a visit of several weeks.

Waymarking

As is normal with German touring trails, the route is superbly waymarked. The signs to follow bear the legend "Romantische Strasse" and show a picture of a bicycle. They are found at virtually every place where there is a chance of confusion with regard to which direction to take. Others are placed for the purpose of reassurance along longer stretches.

One slight source of possible confusion is the waymarking in the Tauber valley between Rothenburg and Tauberbischofsheim. Here the Romantic Road follows exactly the same course as the "Liebliches Taubertal" route, whose signs are far more frequently encountered.

Otherwise, almost the only times when the waymarking can be difficult to locate is when leaving the major staging-posts. To avoid any possible confusion, the correct way out of each town is clearly pinpointed at the relevant point in the text of this book.

It is important to bear in mind that the route as described in this book will be subject to change in the coming years. Existing paths will become worn and will have to be replaced by alternatives, while there will hopefully be a gradual increase in the amount of specially laid track, which will make the route even more attractive for cyclists and walkers.

In cases of dubiety, the best advice is always to follow any waymarkings that are encountered: these are certain to be more current than those described in this book or marked on any map.

Equipment

The Romantic Road is a low-level route which should present no difficulties whatsoever to anyone who is in reasonable physical shape. Only in its sheer length can it be regarded as any kind of challenge, and no special equipment of any kind is required.

In Germany, where there is a long and well-established concern about environmental protection, both cycling and walking are enormously popular mainstream pastimes which are very well catered for, with many special arrangements available.

Cyclists who do not wish to bring their own machine will find it easy enough to rent one once in Germany. The most convenient place to do so is at a railway station: throughout the summer bikes can be hired at very reasonable rates at the left luggage offices of the main stations of most major towns and cities. They can be returned at any other participating station, and can also be taken on most trains, exceptions being the luxury ICE, IC and EC services.

As much of the route is paved, many walkers will find trainers or other soft shoes kinder on the feet than hiking boots, though this is very much a matter of personal preference. It is advisable, however, to wear boots for any ventures into the Alps (eg. the trail up the Tegelberg from Schloss Neuschwanstein), and for the recommended diversion through the Ammerleite on the journey between Rottenbuch and Peiting.

Travel from Britain

By air: Either Frankfurt or Munich can be used as the gateway to the Romantic Road, and both are serviced by regular scheduled flights from London (from where there are several departures every day), Edinburgh, Glasgow, Manchester and Birmingham. The main disadvantage in flying is that the dates and times for both outward and homeward flights have to be fixed in advance, and, once booked, cannot be changed without incurring a hefty penalty.

By rail: The train is unlikely to offer any financial savings; indeed it is usually slightly more expensive. However, not only is there the advantage of being able to buy a ticket right through to the desired end destination, there is also great flexibility: journeys can be made at any time during the two month period of validity, and stopovers can be made at will.

By coach: By far the cheapest option is the coach service from London to either Frankfurt or Munich, though savings have to be balanced against the compensatory discomfort of such a long journey in a confined space. There are several departures each week (the exact number being dependent on the time of year), and open returns are available.

Once in Germany, it is easy enough to catch a train to either of the Romantic Road's two termini. Füssen lies at the end of a branch railway which has direct services to and from Munich and Augsburg on alternate hours. Würzburg is on one of the express lines between Frankfurt and Munich, with very frequent connections to both.

Public transport along the Romantic Road

Germany operates an extremely efficient and well-integrated public transport policy which eschews the concept of competition and relies heavily on subsidies. The railway network, run by the national company Deutsche Bahn (DB), forms the mainstay of the system. Services are very regular, with the normal minimum frequency being hourly on main routes, or once every two hours on rural lines, though in some cases these are reduced at weekends. Buses, whether run by private companies or regional co-operatives, fill the gaps in the system, but run far more sporadically, with three or four services per day being the norm.

Given the well-deserved reputation of the German public

transport network, it is somewhat ironic that it requires considerable dedication and planning to travel the Romantic Road by this means - which is one more reason for choosing to see it by bike or on foot. The only parts of the route which run roughly parallel to rail lines are those between Landsberg and Augsburg and on to Nördlingen, and between Weikersheim and Tauberbischofsheim. No fewer than eleven of the official staging-posts (Schwangau, Steingaden, Wildsteig, Rottenbuch, Hohenfurch, Wallerstein, Dinkelsbühl, Feuchtwangen, Schillingsfürst, Creglingen and Röttingen) are not served by regular passenger trains, while four others (Füssen, Peiting, Schongau and Rothenburg ob der Tauber) are on dead-end branch lines. Although local buses always provide the necessary links, the frequency of service sometimes drops as low as two per day and none at all on Sundays.

Between 1st April and 31st October, however, Europabus runs a daily service in each direction along the entire length of the Romantic Road, pulling a trailer in which bicycles can be carried. One of the northbound buses leaves Füssen at 8am and travels along the official route to Dinkelsbühl, arriving there at 1pm to meet up with a bus which started out from Munich at 9am. The latter then proceeds onwards along the Romantic Road to Würzburg, where it arrives at 6.30pm, before continuing to Frankfurt am Main, where it terminates. The southbound bus leaves Frankfurt at 8am and Würzburg at 10am, arriving at Dinkelsbühl around 3.30pm. It continues onwards to Augsburg and then to Munich, though there is the option of transferring to a second bus, which follows the Romantic Road all the way to Füssen, arriving at 9pm.

The Europabus is of very limited use for short journeys, but it offers a convenient means of making a one-way journey along the Romantic Road. It is therefore particularly useful for anyone who, having walked or cycled the whole route, requires to return to Munich or Frankfurt to catch a plane home. Advance reservations, which are always advisable and sometimes essential, can be made via Deutsche Touring, Am Römerhof, Frankfurt am Main, Tel. (0 69) 7 90 32 56. Those wishing to transport bikes must give a minimum of three days' advance notice.

Maps

For a journey by bike or on foot along the Romantic Road, the spiral-bound "Radroute Romantische Strasse" (1:75,000), which is readily available in tourist offices and bookshops, is an indispensable companion. Laid out on 18 separate sheets, it charts all the twists and turns of the official marked route clearly and unambiguously (save for one very glaring lapse on p.12, where the line is plotted through the middle of the River Lech, rather than along its right bank). The first printing, which dates from 1994, follows exactly the same course as the route described in this book, though it omits some of the variants. Future editions will hopefully correct the aforementioned error and a few other misprints, and incorporate the changes which will inevitably be made to the course of the route.

If more detailed information is required, there are plenty of regional hiking and/or cycling maps with scales of 1:50,000, 1:33,000 or 1:25,000. The town plans handed out by tourist offices are nearly always adequate (and often much more than that), though it is often a good idea to invest in fully comprehensive maps with A-Z listings.

Post offices and telephones

German post offices are normally open Monday to Friday, 8am to 6pm, and Saturday 8am to noon. Mail services to and from the UK normally take from two to four days. Poste restante facilities are available at the main post office of any given town at the counter marked Postlagernde Sendungen.

International telephone calls can be made from all kiosks except those clearly labelled as "National". Many have been adapted to accept magnetic cards, which can be purchased at post offices and newsagents; others accept coins of DM0.10, DM1 and DM5. To call the UK, dial 00 44 and then the subscriber's number, taking care to omit the initial 0.

Public holidays

The following public holidays are observed in Southern Germany:

New Year's Day	(1st January)
Epiphany	(6th January)
Good Friday	
Easter Monday	

May Day	(1st May)
Ascension Day	
Whit Monday	
Corpus Christi	
Feast of the Assumption	(15th August)
Day of German Unity	(3rd October)
All Saints' Day	(1st November)
Day of Prayer and National Repentance (variable Wednesday in November)	
Christmas Day	(25th December)
Boxing Day	(26th December)

On these days, virtually all shops and most other businesses are shut, though hotels and restaurants are generally exceptions to this rule. Some historic monuments are also closed then, whereas others remain open, usually taking the next day off in lieu.

Money

Germany's currency is the Deutschmark (DM). It comes in notes of DM5, DM10, DM20, DM50, DM100, DM200, DM500 and DM1,000, and coins of DM0.01 (one Pfennig), DM0.02, DM0.05, DM0.10, DM0.50, DM1, DM2 and DM5.

Banks are generally open from at least 9am to noon and 1.30pm to 3.30pm on Mondays to Fridays, and many keep far longer hours. There is usually late opening until 6pm on Thursdays, and some branches also open on Saturday mornings. Most banks will cash travellers' cheques, though the commission levied tends to vary widely. They can also offer cash advances on the credit card company or companies with which they are associated: stickers in the windows indicate which these are.

Credit cards, however, are used far less widely in Germany than in other Western European countries and although an increasing number of hotels, restaurants and shops accept them, many others do not. It is therefore prudent to carry reasonable reserves of ready cash at all times.

In view of the strength of the Deutschmark, it is perhaps surprising that Germany is, for the most part, an affordable country in which to travel. Restaurant prices are, on the whole, lower than in Britain, with the caveat that the concept of the bargain set-priced lunch is not nearly so well established. Accommodation rates also compare quite favourably, particularly in popular holiday areas such as the Alps, where many remarkable bargains can be found.

Health

British citizens, in common with all EU residents, are entitled to free medical treatment in Germany on production of an E111 certificate, which is available from main post offices and DSS offices. Without it, medical charges will have to be paid in full.

It is advisable to carry a small box or bag of medical supplies at all times; this should include such items as elastoplast, antiseptic creams, aspirins, antihistamines and insect repellents. Emergency supplies can be purchased in any pharmacy (Apotheke), which can be found in all but the smallest villages.

Addresses

In German addresses, the name of the street is always written before the number. Strasse (street) is commonly abbreviated to Str., and often joined on to the end of the previous word. Other names, which again are sometimes tacked on to the preceding word, include Allee (Avenue), Brücke (bridge), Gasse (alley), Platz (square), Ring (ring road), Ufer (quay) and Weg (way).

Many villages have been incorporated into the municipality of nearby towns, and in such cases the name of the latter is (in formal usage if not in common parlance) adopted as a prefix. Thus Hohenschwangau, for example, is officially known as Schwangau-Hohenschwangau, Wies as Steingaden-Wies, Detwang as Rothenburg ob der Tauber-Detwang and Stuppach as Bad Mergentheim-Stuppach. Some hamlets and small villages only have house numbers, not street names.

Tourist offices

Each of the Romantic Road's staging-posts has its own tourist office, which can provide full up-to-the-minute local information and help with finding somewhere to stay. Almost invariably, the staff can speak English. Most offices publish an annual prospectus listing and describing virtually all the available accommodation; many also produce monthly lists of events. (See Appendix 3 for a list of all tourist offices on the Romantic Road.)

Opening hours of tourist offices can be fickle, and are often longer in the summer. In the major cities and other popular destinations, expect to find the tourist office open from at least 9am to 6pm on Mondays to Saturdays, but in some of the smaller villages it may close at lunchtimes and from noon on Fridays until Monday morning.

Note that the offices go under many different titles, Tourist-Information, Verkehrsamt, and Fremdenverkehrsamt being the most common. In health resorts, the tourist office is usually incorporated within the visitor reception centre, the Kurverwaltung; in many small towns and villages it is located within the local administration headquarters, the Stadtverwaltung or Gemeindeverwaltung.

The Dinkelsbühl office is also the headquarters of the Touristik-Arbeitgemeinschaft Romantische Strasse, which is responsible for promoting the route as an entity, and is thus the best contact for general enquiries. In the UK, the German National Tourist Office, 65 Curzon Street, London W1Y 7PE, Tel: (0171) 493 0080, has a large stock of brochures on all parts of Germany.

Hotels, inns and pensions

Accommodation in Germany is subject to a somewhat complicated categorization system. The official classification of Hotel is not applied as widely as in many other countries, being confined in the main to mid-range and expensive establishments which offer a full range of facilities, including a restaurant. Those of similar standing which serve no meals other than breakfast are classed as Hotel Garni or Hotel-Pension.

The designation Gasthof signifies a uniquely German institution, roughly equivalent to a traditional inn. As a general rule, its bar-cum-restaurant, which almost invariably has a regular local clientele, forms the mainstay of the business, with the accommodation playing a secondary role.

In complete contrast are establishments with a Pension designation, the nearest equivalent to the British guest-house. These are usually located in large houses or apartment blocks, and serve breakfast but not other meals. In the main resorts - though not in the larger towns and cities - rooms are also available in many private houses on a bed-and-breakfast basis.

It is important to be aware that the provision and range of accommodation on offer along the Romantic Road varies markedly. There is a particularly wide choice in those places (such as Füssen, Schwangau, Rothenburg ob der Tauber and Bad Mergentheim) which are heavily dependent on tourism, and these towns also generally offer the best value for money. Augsburg is unusual among major German cities in being well endowed with accommodation to suit every pocket; Würzburg is more typical in having plenty of medium-range and luxury establishments, but only a few budget options. Peiting, Schongau and Landsberg are noticeably pricier than the villages nearby, or than similarly sized towns elsewhere.

For maximum convenience and flexibility in planning, the list in Appendix 4 covers not only all the official staging-posts along the route, but also a number of places in between. Although selective, particularly in respect of the larger cities and the main resorts, it in many cases includes all the available options, other than private houses, which have been excluded for logistical reasons. For an up-to-date annual list of all available accommodation possibilities, contact the appropriate tourist office. Alternatively, ask for the leaflet "Hotels, Gasthöfe, Pensionen an der Romantischen Strasse", which is updated every other year and is fairly (but not fully) comprehensive in its coverage.

Youth hostels
As befits the birthplace of hostelling, Germany boasts more youth hostels than any other country in the world. It is all the more surprising, therefore, that there are no more than eleven along the Romantic Road. Of these, the seven which are in Bavaria are subject to the provincial rule which restricts access to those under 27 years of age, though exceptions are made for adults accompanying children. No such restraints apply to the four in Baden-Württemberg (Creglingen, Weikersheim, Igersheim and Tauberbischofsheim), but over-27s are charged a slightly higher tariff.

Those wishing to use the hostels must be in possession of a valid IYHF card and the officially approved sheet sleeping bag. The maximum length of stay is three consecutive nights, but this can be extended at the discretion of the warden. Note that hostels are liable to be block-booked by school groups at any time of the year, most frequently on summer weekdays and in weekends out of season. See Appendix 4 for a list of hostels on the Romantic Road.

Campsites

Camping is every bit as well established in Germany as hostelling, and there is a fairly even spread of campsites along the Romantic Road. These are invariably the cheapest available form of accommodation, and are almost always well managed, though it has to be said that camping purists tend to find German sites rather too regimented. Another recurrent snag is that many campsites are located some distance away from the towns they serve, and much time can be wasted in commuting back and forth.

Eating and drinking

German cuisine is notable for its homeliness, not least in the generosity of portions, and in its consistently high standards, which are rigorously maintained almost everywhere, no matter how isolated the location. Among the great pleasures of walking or cycling the Romantic Road are the opportunities it offers for stopping off for lunch or dinner at a traditional Gasthof to enjoy, usually at a very reasonable cost, a hearty meal prepared from the freshest ingredients washed down with a glass or two of locally produced beer or wine.

Breakfast (Frühstück) is almost invariably included in the price of a room, regardless of what category of accommodation is chosen. In most cases, what is offered falls midway between the spartan start to the day favoured in France and the elaborate Scandinavian cold table. Typically, a small platter of cold meats (Aufschnittplatte), most of them sausage-based, and cheese (Käse) is presented, along with jam (Marmelade) and honey (Honig). Muesli or another cereal is sometimes included as well, or as an alternative to the platter, while in country areas a fresh boiled egg (Gekochtes Ei) is often served. There is generally a variety of different types of bread (Brot), including such national favourites as the dark rye-based Pumpernickel and the salted Brezel. Both brown and white rolls are popular, and often have an added condiment, such as caraway, coriander, poppy or sesame seeds.

Coffee (Kaffee), which is normally freshly brewed, is the normal breakfast accompaniment. Tea (Tee) is growing in popularity, but the weak blends favoured in Germany do not mix well with milk, and are best drunk either straight (Schwarz) or with lemon (mit Zitrone). Herbal infusions (Kräutertee or Pflanzentee) and hot chocolate (Trinkschockolade) are popular alternatives. Orange juice (Orangensaft) is sometimes included as well.

Just as the British have morning and afternoon tea, so do the Germans have their coffee and cakes (Kaffee und Kuchen). Though the elegant Café-Konditorei - where a choice of espresso, capuccino and mocha is served as an accompaniment to cream cakes (Sahnetorten), pastries (Gebäck) or handmade chocolates (Schockoladen) - is an institution normally associated with Austria, it is every bit as popular in Germany, with at least one in any fair-sized village.

Germans are very flexible about the main meal of the day. Many favour a heavy lunch (Mittagessen), eaten at any time between 11.30am and 2pm, and therefore require only a light supper (Abendbrot), usually at around 7pm. Others, however, favour a light lunch and a heavy dinner (Abendessen). All restaurants must by law display their menus and prices at the door, together with a note saying which day, if any, they are closed (Ruhetag). An increasing number offer a bargain daily menu (Tageskarte) of two or three courses, which is usually but not necessarily available at lunchtimes only. Those serving hot food throughout the day normally have a sign saying "durchgehend warme Kuche". Despite the inroads made by Neue Deutsche Kuche, the German version of nouvelle cuisine, most practise the homely traditional cooking style known as Gutburgerliche Kuche. Most inns have a hard core of local customers who sit at tables marked "Stammtisch". Unless invited to do so, it is not the done thing to sit at one of these. Tables are often very large, and sharing is normal practice at busy periods.

Many favourite soups are adaptations or copies of foreign models. These include a liquidized form of the Hungarian goulash (Ungarische Goulaschsuppe), a brown French onion soup with cheese and croutons (Französische Zwiebelsuppe), and a spicy

Serbian-inspired bean soup (Serbische Bohnensuppe). More authentically Bavarian are the clear stock-based soups with floating liver dumplings (Leberknödelsuppe), egg (Bouillon mit Ei), or pancake strips (Flädlesuppe or Pfannkuchensuppe). Franconian specialities include a soup made with wine and cream (Fränkische Weinsuppe). Most of the commonly encountered alternatives are vegetable-based, though vegetarians should beware that bones and fat are often used in the cooking. Starters other than soups are fairly rudimentary: melon with ham (Melone mit Schinken), salad (Salat), paté (Pastete) and plates of cold cuts similar to those found on breakfast tables.

Main courses are overwhelmingly pork-based (vom Schwein), though this is less restricting than it might appear, as virtually every part of the pig is used and prepared in a seemingly limitless variety of ways. Thus, for example, a Schnitzel may be served plain (Naturschnitzel), with a coating of breadcrumbs (Wiener Schnitzel), smothered with mushrooms (Jägerschnitzel), or with a fiery sauce of red and green peppers (Zigeunerschnitzel). As an alternative to the ubiquitous pork schnitzel, chop (Kotelett) and steak (Steak), try the knuckle or trotter, which is both filling and tasty. It can be had either boiled (Eisbein) or else roasted or grilled (Schweinehaxe). Sausages (Wurst) regularly feature on menus, and are often regarded as items of serious cuisine. There are many regional varieties, one Bavarian speciality being white sausage (Weisswurst), which is traditionally eaten as a pre-lunch snack.

Beef (Rind) and veal (Kalb) are far less popular than pork, and generally much more expensive. Chicken (Hähnchen or Huhn) is by far the most commonly encountered form of poultry (Geflügel), and is often the cheapest main course on the menu. Spit-roasting is the favourite method of preparation, though fricassee on a bed of rice (Reis) is also popular.

A fair number of restaurants, particularly in rural areas, serve game dishes, including more exotic poultry such as goose (Gans), duck (Ente) and pheasant (Fasan) as well as venison (Hirsch or Reh), rabbit (Kanninchen) and hare (Hase). Because Southern Germany is so far from the sea, fish (Fisch) dishes tend to be of the freshwater variety. Trout (Forelle) is the most common; others include the more expensive carp (Karp), pike (Hecht) and pike-perch (Zander).

The price of a main course almost invariably includes vegetables. True to the national stereotype, cabbage (Kohl or Kraut), both hot and cold, takes pride of place. The red kind is normally stewed with apple (Apfelrotkohl) or served cold with vinegar (Rotkohlsalat), while its green counterpart is pickled with juniper berries (Sauerkraut) or else made into a coleslaw salad (Krautsalat). Potatoes (Kartoffeln) are similarly ubiquitous, and are usually sautéd (Bratkartoffeln), boiled (Salzkartoffeln), creamed (Kartoffelpuree) or else served as French fries (Pommes Frites) or mixed with mayonnaise into a potato salad (Kartoffelsalat). Dumplings made from potatoes and flour (Kartoffelknödeln) are also common, as are those made from bread and herbs (Semmelknödeln).

Among other vegetables, mushrooms (Pilze), and in particular the wild woodland varieties, are especially delicious, and are often served as main courses in season. Salads of lettuce (Kopfsalat), tomatoes (Tomaten), cucumber (Gurken), gherkins (Gewürzgurken), beetroot (Rote Rube) and carrots (Mohren) are often served as a side-dish to supplement the vegetables on the main plate. Noodles (Nudeln) are a key component of the distinctive regional cuisine of Swabia, and are often encountered in neighbouring areas as well. The shredded Spätzle is served either as an accompaniment, or else cooked with cheese to form a main dish in its own right (Käsespätzle). Maultaschen are parcels of finely chopped meat and herbs, broadly similar in style to ravioli.

Desserts in restaurants seldom compare with the offerings available in a Café-Konditorei. Following on from hefty main courses, they are almost invariably cold and light, functioning more as a palate cleanser than as a climax to the meal. Many are fruit-based and those with berries (Beeren), particularly when mixed together in a compote (Kompott), are particularly refreshing. Bavaria does, however, have a hot and heavy alternative to these in the steamed yeast dumpling (Dampfnudel), which is usually smothered in a custard-like vanilla sauce.

The German national drink is beer (Bier): the country has around 40% of the world's breweries, with some 800 (about half the total) in Bavaria alone. Many distinctive varieties of beer are produced, and virtually every restaurant can offer several of these on tap (vom Fass), with others available in bottles (Flaschenbiere).

In the case of the former, there is often a choice of measures: these usually range between 0.3 litre and 0.5 litre, though in Bavaria it is often possible to order a full 1 litre measure (Mass).

A Pils is a bottom-fermented golden-coloured beer with a very high hop content; an Export is slightly stronger and sweeter. Weizenbier (or Weissbier), which is produced by the old-fashioned top-fermenting method, is made from wheat and has a tart, refreshing taste. It is available either with the yeast sediment left in (Hefe-Weizen), or taken out (Kristall-Weizen); the former can be quite heady, while the latter is light and sparkling, earning it the nickname of the "champagne of beers". Bockbier is a strong beer containing at least 6.25% alcohol, a figure which is increased for special festive brews such as Doppelbock and Maibock. Hell signifies that a beer is light in colour, Dunkel that it is dark (and hence slightly sweet). Spezial denotes a premier product, whereas a Vollbier is a standard type. Beer mixed with lemonade is known as Radler (literally, "cyclist").

In its Franconian stretch, the Romantic Road passes through one of Germany's leading wine (Wein) regions. As the climate does not ripen red grapes regularly, most of its vintages are white (weiss), the exception being Spätburgunder, which is red (rot). The most common grape varieties are Müller-Thurgau, which is mild in acidity and has an aromatic, flowery bouquet; Silvaner, which is sturdy and full-bodied with more acidity but a light bouquet; and the highly prestigious Riesling, which has a floral aroma when young, often becomes honeyed when ripe, and develops a fruity bouquet after several years in the bottle. Other types include the hybrids Kerner, Scheurebe and Bacchus.

Wines, whether from Franconia or other German wine regions such as Baden, the Mosel or the Rhineland, can be ordered by the glass in most restaurants. If buying in a shop, Franconian wines are easy to spot, as they come in a distinctively dumpy, round-shouldered bottle (Bocksbeutel). The best vintages are clearly labelled as "Qualitätswein mit Prädikat" (Quality wine with special attribute). These are divided into several categories, Kabinett being the lightest and lowest in alcohol. Spätlese is made from fully matured grapes, Auslese from the choicest grapes, Beerenauslese from individually picked late harvested grapes, and Trockenbeerenauslese from grapes

27

left on the vine until some of their water content has evaporated.

Drinks for rounding off a meal include Korn, a fiery rye-based spirit, and Weinbrand, the German form of brandy; milder alternatives include various fruit-based liqueurs. In winter, hot rum with sugar (Grog) and mulled wine with spices (Glühwein) are good ways of warding off a cold. The most popular soft drinks are apple juice (Apfelsaft), grape juice (Traubensaft), and lemonade (Zitronenlimonade). Mineral water (Mineralwasser) generally comes from one of the multitude of German spas.

Picnicking is likely to be only marginally cheaper than eating in a restaurant, but may sometimes be necessary on the longer stretches of the route. Even the smaller villages have well-stocked grocers' stores, which are usually laid out in the manner of a supermarket, making it easy for foreign visitors who do not know the language to select their desired purchases. In the larger villages and towns, an extremely appetizing picnic can be put together from a visit to a supermarket or a trip round the local baker, butcher and grocer.

Festivals and folklore

Germany probably has more annual festivals than any other European country, and nowhere is the habit of celebration stronger than in the south of the country. Almost every village has its annual summer fair (variously known as Sommerfest, Volksfest, Heimatfest or Bürgerfest), and there is also a rich mixture of religious, pagan, folklore, music, wine and beer festivals which together fill the entire calendar.

In the course of a journey along the Romantic Road, it is well worth trying to experience some of the festivals held along the route. As only a few of these have firmly fixed dates, it is best to check the exact times in advance. A useful free leaflet "Veranstaltungen an der Romantischen Strasse", published annually and available from any of the tourist offices along the route, gives the exact dates for that year of most (though not all) of the festivals. For more detailed information on any specific event, it is advisable to contact the local tourist office.

Listed in Appendix 5 is a selection of the festivals, along with fixed or approximate dates and short descriptions where appropriate. The costumed events are particularly worth seeing: Germans love nothing better than to don historic dress and process through the streets of their town on foot, on horseback or in enormous floats. Such festivals are important expressions of the strong community spirit that has always been a feature of life in Germany's smaller towns and villages. Almost invariably, they are meticulously planned and prepared, are enacted with superb aplomb, and are wonderfully photogenic. Tents serving special festive beer and food are nearly always featured.

A selected list of the festivals along the Romantic Road which have gained a national reputation would certainly include the Colomansfest in Schwangau, the Ruethenfest in Landsberg, the Stabenfest and Scharlachrennen in Nördlingen, the Kinderzech' - Festwoche in Dinkelsbühl, the Reichstadtfesttage in Rothenburg, and the Kilianifest in Würzburg.

One other folklore tradition worth mentioning is that of the nightwatchman: the Romantic Road's three famous walled towns of Nördlingen, Dinkelsbühl and Rothenburg ob der Tauber are among the last places in Europe to maintain this post, though in each the nightwatchmen perform a completely different function.

In Nördlingen, they act as year-round custodians of the main watchtower, the Danielturm of the Georgskirche, sounding the watch every half-hour between 10pm and midnight. The Dinkelsbühl nightwatchman, on the other hand, is employed only from April to October each year. Decked out in cloak, breeches and felt hat, and carrying a halberd, horn and a lantern, he departs from the Georgskirche at 9pm (9.30pm in July and August) and does the rounds of many of the town's hotels and inns. At each, having performed his song "Hört ihr Leut" ("Listen, you people"), he is rewarded with a glass of wine, which is passed around the tourists accompanying him. His Rothenburg counterpart - who likewise wears anachronistic garb and works only in the April to October tourist season - acts as a guide. He leads English-language tours round the town at 8pm, then does the same tour in German at 9.30pm.

Füssen

The southern terminus of the Romantic Road is **FÜSSEN**, which lies hard by the Austrian border, and at the end of a branch rail line with regular direct services to both Munich and Augsburg. It makes a fitting beginning or ending to the route, as it is magnificently sited at the conjunction of the two main landscapes of the Allgäu region - the plateau, with its meadows, lakes, moorland and coniferous and deciduous woodland; and the towering Alpine chain of the Ammergebirge (Ammer mountains). This juxtaposition of scenery is reflected in the character of the Lech, a recurrent landmark throughout the first half of the Romantic Road: within the town's boundaries it changes from a mountain stream into an impressively broad river.

The site of Füssen is known to have been inhabited in the Stone Age, and in Roman times a settlement, known as Foetibus, was established there. In the 8th century, the missionary monk St Magnus built his hermitage there, and around 850 a Benedictine monastery was founded on the same site. Füssen gained town rights in 1295, and in 1313 was incorporated into the territory of the Augsburg Prince-Bishopric. It had its heyday in the 15th and 16th centuries, when it enjoyed commercial prosperity and regular Imperial patronage but, like so many other German towns, went into steep decline during the Thirty Years' War of 1618-48.

In 1803 it was allocated to the erstwhile duchy of Bavaria, which at the same time was raised to the rank of a fully fledged kingdom, a status it maintained until 1918, despite its absorption in 1871 into the Prussian-dominated Second German Reich. The 19th century saw Füssen's fortunes recover, thanks to the onset of industrialization and to the building nearby of the two great royal castles, Schloss Hohenschwangau and Schloss Neuschwanstein.

Nowadays, tourism is a key component of the local economy of the town, whose municipal area - which includes the resort villages of Bad Faulenbach, Weissensee and Hopfen am See - now has a population of some 16,000. Although foreigners flock to Füssen in droves, most are short-stay visitors who use the town as a base for a trip to the royal castles, which rank among the most popular tourist attractions in Europe. German holidaymakers, in contrast, tend to come for much longer stays, whether for skiing in winter, or in summer for exploring the 180km of hiking trails which are to be found in the vicinity. Others come to Füssen for a Kneipp cure, a specialized hydropathic treatment which also includes herbal and dietary remedies, plus both rest and exercise.

Füssen's historic core lies just south-east of the railway station. Its main shopping street is the pedestrianized Reichenstrasse, towards the northern end of which is the church of St Nikolaus (St Nicholas), popularly known as the **Krippkirche** ("Crib Church"). This was built for the Jesuits in 1717 by Johann Jakob Herkomer, a talented local Baroque architect, painter and interior decorator. The high altar is thought to be an early work of a far more celebrated architect, Dominikus Zimmermann, whose masterpiece, the Wieskirche, is one of the highlights of the Romantic Road.

Rather than continuing along Reichenstrasse, it is worth making a short detour along the quieter alleys to the east, which are likewise free of traffic. At the end of Schrannengasse, which frames the facade of the Krippkirche, is a gabled Gothic house, known as the **Vogtei** (Governor's Office), in honour of the function it served under the Augsburg Prince-Bishopric. Diagonally opposite, at the head of Brunnengasse, is the **Kornhaus** (Granary), which dates from 1483. Further down Brunnengasse is the **Sturmhaus**, the home and workshop of the Baroque sculptor Anton Sturm, who carved the relief over the entrance showing the Madonna and infant Jesus being worshipped by St Anthony of Padua, St Johann Nepomuk, an angel and a child.

At the end of Brunnengasse, Hutergasse leads to the wide open space at the bottom end of Reichenstrasse, from where there is a fine view of the northern elevation of the **Hohes Schloss** (High Castle), which stands above a sheer drop on the hill above. The original fortress was constructed between 1293 and 1323, but was rebuilt in late Gothic style between 1490 and 1503 in order to serve as a summer residence of the Augsburg Prince-Bishops, and consequently combines defensive and palatial features. A key feature of its silhouette is the Uhrturm (Clocktower) at the north-eastern corner, which served as a prison and as the home and look-out of the watchman. From the corner oriel, it was possible to survey the entire medieval town. The other oriel was used for pouring moulten lead on attackers, who were forced to approach via what is still the only means of access: from the rear through the outer defensive wall.

In an ingenious cost-saving device, the inner courtyard is adorned with illusionistic early 16th century paintings showing elaborate door and window frames and oriels. Most of the Schloss is now used as offices, but part of the north wing has been adapted to house a branch of the **Bayerische Staatsgalerie** (Bavarian State Gallery). Paintings by 15th and 16th century South German masters and members of the 19th century Munich School are on view, but the main attraction is the Rittersaal (Knights' Hall), with its elaborate coffered vault.

Immediately below the Schloss is the massive complex of the former **Kloster St Mang** (St Magnus' Monastery). Its present appearance is almost entirely the result of a Baroque rebuilding carried out between 1701 and 1726 under Johann Jakob Herkomer, but a few older features were retained. Among these is the Romanesque tower of the church: now the **Stadtpfarrkirche** (Town Parish Church).

St Magnus' grave is in the **Krypta** (crypt), a rare surviving example of the pre-Romanesque architecture of the Carolingian period. It dates back at least as far as the 9th century, and part of the fabric may even have existed in the saint's lifetime. The fresco, showing St Magnus in the company of St Gall, was painted around 980. Although the crypt is accessible on Sunday mornings, it can otherwise only be seen by guided tours which are held once or twice per week; the times for these are posted in the church's porch.

Adjoining the church is the **Annakapelle** (St Anne's Chapel). Its foundations are Carolingian, and it was probably the original monastic church, later being converted to serve as the funerary chapel of the nobility of the Füssen region.

The Annakapelle, and the excavations of the Romanesque cloisters alongside, can only be seen as part of a visit to the **Museum der Stadt Füssen** (Museum of the Town of Füssen); access to this is via the main monastic courtyard, whose entry is round the corner on Lechhalde. This has displays on the history of the monastery and

View of the Alps, the Alpsee and Schloss Hohenschwangau from
Schloss Neuschwanstein
Schloss Neuschwanstein, seen from the Marienbrücke

The River Ammer below Rottenbuch
Schongau, the Polizeidienerturm and houses built over the Stadtmaue

the town, with a special section on the local manufacture of lutes and violins, which began in the 16th and 17th centuries respectively.

Further down Lechhalde is the Rococo **Heilig-Geist-Spitalkirche** (Holy Ghost Hospital Church), built in 1748-9 by a local architect, Franz Karl Fischer, as a replacement for its fire-ravaged Gothic predecessor. Its facade is an outstanding example of the distinctively Bavarian style of exterior mural painting known as Lüftlmalerei, a uniquely Roman Catholic art form which had its roots in the heightened religious zeal bequeathed by the Counter-Reformation. Between the window are portraits of the patron saints of water, St Florian and St Christopher, while on the lower part of the two-tiered gable is a representation of the Holy Trinity. It is well worth crossing over the Lech via the bridge to the rear of the church; from the opposite bank is a fine view of the town, and in particular of the Kloster St Mang.

From the Heilig-Geist-Spitalkirche, follow Spitalgasse east, turn right into Flossergasse, then left into Stadtbleiche, which is entered via a passageway known as the **Bleichertörle**. Over its Gothic arch is a sandstone relief dated 1503 bearing the coat-of-arms of Prince-Bishop Friedrich von Zollern, the builder of the Hohes Schloss. On the high ground above is the **Franziskanerkloster** (Franciscan Monastery), built in the 1760s by Franz Karl Fischer in a surprisingly sober Baroque style. Behind it stretches the only surviving section of the **Stadtmauer** (Town Wall), which includes three towers, a gateway and the sentry walk. This is seen to best effect from the **Alter Friedhof** (Old Cemetery), whose entrance is beside the part-Gothic, part-Baroque church of **St Sebastian** on Klosterstrasse to the north.

Those wishing to explore beyond the historic centre should follow Sebastianstrasse eastwards, turning north immediately before the bridge into Lechuferweg, which leads along the bank of the river to the harbour at the end of the **Forggensee**. This huge reservoir, the largest of the many lakes in the vicinity, was created in 1954. It is 12km long, up to 3km wide and has an area of 16.5km. From 15th June until the beginning of October it is open for public bathing, sailing and angling. Throughout this period, two steamers ply the lake, offering a choice of 50-minute or 2-hour cruises.

Another destination just a short walk or cycle ride from the centre of Füssen is the formerly separate village of **BAD FAULENBACH**, which can be reached on foot from the Hohes Schloss in about 10 minutes via the Baumgarten, a wooded park on the hillside above the Lech. As its prefix indicates, Bad Faulenbach has the official status of a fully fledged spa resort, one which offers a variety of thermal and mud baths in addition to the Kneipp cures which are available in Füssen itself. A typically quiet, soporific district, it has two small lakes, the Mittersee and the Obersee, each with open-air swimming facilities, at its western edge. At the opposite end of the suburb, Ländeweg leads down through the woods to a renowned beauty spot, the **Lechfall**. In addition to the waterfall, there is a short but surprisingly wild-looking gorge - the only one on any of the major Alpine rivers.

The first stage of the Romantic Road, from Füssen to Schwangau via the royal castles at Hohenschwangau, is just 6km in length. However, the scenery is easily the most glorious to be seen on the entire route, some detours are essential, and others hard to resist. One day is the absolute minimum required to see the chief attractions, and only the most rushed visitor could possibly refrain from staying longer. Because the distances are so short, there is no real need to change the overnight base for covering this stage, and in this connection it is worth considering either Hohenschwangau or Schwangau as an alternative to Füssen.

The official Romantic Road cycle- and footpath leaves Füssen by the Sebastianstrasse, crossing the Lech by the small bridge adjacent to that which carries the main B17 road out of town. From there, look backwards to enjoy a fine view over the river and the historic town centre. The path continues eastwards, running parallel to the right-hand side of the busy B310 road, also known as Parkstrasse. Its shady, tree-lined course offers some welcome relief from the relentless pounding of cars and tourist coaches bound for the royal castles.

Immediately beyond the hamlet of Alterschrofen, which is skirted by Parkstrasse, there is the opportunity of escaping from the tourist hordes altogether by making a detour south into the **Schwanseepark**, a landscaped park laid out on marshy moorland in 1852-3 in the naturalistic "English" style. It is planted with a host of imported trees and shrubs, so arranged to present beautifully framed vistas of the castles. Several paths, all suitable for both walking and cycling, lead from the main route into the park. The first of these is immediately beyond Königstrasse, a road linking Altershrofen with the Füssen suburb of Zieglwies on the south bank of the Lech.

At the heart of the park is the **Schwansee** itself, which is encircled by a 2km long path providing magnificent views of the castles and the Ammergebirge chain. *Its name literally means "Swan Lake" in honour of the fact that swans live there throughout the year. The aloof serenity of these birds has cast a spell on rulers of the area down the centuries. In the Middle Ages, they were adopted as the emblem of the local knights, and the very name of Hohenschwangau, which they adopted for their realm, means "High Country of the Swan". The 19th century Bavarian kings Maximilian II and his son Ludwig II were obsessed with the swan motif and the medieval Grail legends associated with it, as the decoration of their castles bears witness.*

From the south-eastern tip of the Schwansee, a marked pathway leads uphill to Pindarplatz, where the local lodge of Alpine hornblowers practises every Monday evening in summer. It lies directly above a much larger and deeper lake, the **Alpsee**, which is likewise circumnavigated by a path suitable for both walking and cycling. With the exception of some 200m immediately east of Pindarplatz, the path closely hugs the shore along its entire 6km length, and offers yet more wonderful panoramas. In contrast to the Schwansee, which is a strict nature reserve, the waters of the Alpsee are accessible for acquatic pursuits in summer: pleasure boats can be hired from the south

shore jetty just beyond the eastern tip of the lake, while there are open-air swimming facilities midway along the same shore.

Despite the fact that it is no more than a hamlet, **HOHENSCHWANGAU** is nonetheless the most rampantly commercialized place in the whole of Germany. No fewer than five capacious car parks (where cycles can also be left) are dotted around an assortment of souvenir shops, hotels, guesthouses, restaurants

STAGES 1 & 2

Wieskirche

Trauchgau

Berghof

Halblech

Bayernniederhofen

Buching

Bannwaldsee

vangau

Wallfahrtskirche

† St Coloman

hrofen

Tegelbergbahn

▲ Schloss Neuschwanstein

Hohenschwangau

chloss Hohenschwangau

and snack bars, plus a tourist office and a post office. Those following the direct 4km route from Füssen will arrive in the middle of the village, where Parkstrasse meets with three other roads. Of these, Schwangauer Strasse leads north-west to Schwangau, Colomannstrasse northwards to the Wallfahrtskirche St Coloman, and Alpseestrasse the short distance south to the Alpsee.

The smaller and older of the two royal castles is the golden yellow **Schloss Hohenschwangau**, which stands at an elevation of 850m almost directly above the western shore of the Alpsee. There

37

are three means of access on foot, the quickest taking about eight minutes by the steepish pathway from the car park on Alpseestrasse. It takes about twice that time via either the woodland path from the road junction, or the tarmac road from Pindarplatz.

In the 12th century, the local knights erected a fortress on the spot, and in its early years this was a centre for the courtly troubadour tradition known in Germany as Minnesang. When the knights died out in the 16th century, their castle fell into decay, and it was rendered totally ruinous in the Napoleonic Wars. Maximilian II, while still Crown Prince, purchased the site and commissioned a theatre designer, Domenic Quaglio, to build a replacement castle, which was erected between 1832 and 1836. The result is a Romantic fantasy which shows an obvious debt to the English Tudor style, which was then much in vogue in Germany. Despite this, the new Schloss was intended as an evocation of the medieval German troubadour past, and as a glorification of the Wittelsbach dynasty, which had ruled Bavaria without interruption since 1180. The building remains in family hands to this day.

There is free access to the terraced gardens, which command a fine view across to Schloss Neuschwanstein. They contain several fountains, including one in the shape of a swan, a recurrent motif throughout the Schloss. Entry to the interior is by guided tour only. Although English as well as German versions of this are available, they are subject to demand and are spasmodic outside the high season, as it seems that only a minority of overseas tourists choose to visit the interior.

Ludwig's own **Schloss Neuschwanstein**, *the ultimate fantasy castle, has become Germany's most famous tourist icon. Its image - a brilliant white confection bristling with battlements, towers, turrets and pinnacles and nestling among Alpine peaks, forests and lakes - has become famous the world over as a result of its appearance in countless books, brochures and posters, and it has served as the direct inspiration for the theme park castles pioneered by the Walt Disney Corporation, which featured Neuschwanstein itself in the film "Chitty Chitty Bang Bang".*

Begun in 1869, it inaugurated a building programme which included two further royal palaces: Linderhof near Oberammergau and Herrenchiemsee on an island in the Chiemsee. These grandiose buildings were intended not so much as expressions of the power and magnificence of Bavaria and its ruling house, but rather as the fulfilment of Ludwig's personal dreams and self-image.

As such, Neuschwanstein functioned as a tribute to medieval German chivalry; to the composer Richard Wagner, who had evoked this past so intoxicatingly in his vast music dramas; and to Ludwig's belief in himself as a divinely chosen king to whom the inner mysteries of the Holy Grail had been revealed. Thus Neuschwanstein was planned as a fusion of the legendary Holy Grail castle of Monsalvat and of the real-life Wartburg, the great medieval fortress in Thuringia where the famous German troubadour contest described in Wagner's "Tannhäuser" was held in 1207.

Ludwig chose the site of the ruined castle of Vorderhohenschwangau, which his father had intended to rebuild, as the setting for this extravaganza. In a letter to Wagner he wrote, "The spot is one of the most beautiful that one could ever find, sacred and out of reach". These last words now sound richly ironic, given that nowadays there are two million paying visitors each year. A further irony is that these visitors make the castle a money-spinning operation for the state of Bavaria, one which has paid for itself many times over. Yet it was the crippling costs of this and other royal palaces that led to Ludwig's ministers plotting to have him declared insane. The news was conveyed to the king in June 1886 by a commission sent to Neuschwanstein. He was escorted to Schloss Berg on the Starnberger See near Munich, where he died a couple of days later in mysterious circumstances which have never been satisfactorily explained.

Although the artistic worth of Schloss Neuschwanstein is much disputed, there can be no doubt about the audacity and verve of the design, which relies on a symbiotic relationship with the landscapes surrounding the levelled rocky outcrop of the site. These have a stark duality: to the west, there is the open plateau, while to the east lies the dark, brooding expanse of the Pöllatschlucht, with the massive peak of Säuling (2047m), which is often shrouded in mist, rearing up behind.

The initial plans for the Schloss were drawn up by a Munich theatre designer, Christian Jank, with the close collaboration of the king. A stage set previously used for Wagner's "Tannhäuser" served as the basis for the overall silhouette, while another one for "Lohengrin" was followed in the design of the main courtyard. Professional architects - successively Eduard Riedel, Georg Dollmann and Julius Hofmann - were only called in to supervise the actual construction.

Standing at an elevation of 964m, Neuschwanstein is a fairly stiff 20 minute walk up from Hohenschwangau via the quickest route, the walking trail from the car park at the southern end of

Colomannstrasse; the gentler ascent by Neuschwansteinstrasse, the tarmac road at the southern end of Alpseestrasse, takes a good 10 minutes longer. Admission to the interior is by guided tour, and tickets are sold only at the booth between the Schlosswirtschaft restaurant and the Schloss itself. From there, take the left fork to the red sandstone entrance gateway, the first part to be built, and the only contrast to the building's otherwise relentless grey-white granite. Even out of season there are often horrendously long queues for admission, and it therefore makes sense to come as early as possible. At the busiest periods, an estimate of the likely waiting time is posted up.

Once inside the building, visitors are shepherded up to the fourth floor, where separate queues are formed for tours in German and English. Because of the sheer pressure of numbers, the guides rush round in 35 minutes, which unfortunately means that there is little time to examine the interior decorations in detail, or to wallow in the breathtaking series of panoramas of the surrounding countryside from the balconies. There is, however, the opportunity to linger over the famous picture postcard view southwards over Schloss Hohenschwangau, the Alpsee and the Schwansee from the staircase on the way out.

On the fourth floor, the main chamber is the Thronsaal (Throne Hall), which has the appearance of a Byzantine church, with brilliantly colourful decoration symbolizing Ludwig's self-image as a King of the Holy Grail. The ceiling, which supports a huge wheel-shaped chandelier, is painted to resemble the sky, complete with stars and sun, while the mosaic floor, made from over two million stones, has representations of the animal and plant kingdoms, signifying the earth. The private apartments of the king on the same floor are decorated with paintings in the grand Historicist manner by a team of Munich artists, of whom Ferdinand Piloty was the most accomplished. Almost the whole of the fifth storey is occupied by the Sängersaal (Singers' Hall), which features a cycle of paintings illustrating Wagner's valedictory "Parsifal"; a stage set of "Klingsor's Magic Forest" by Christian Jank; and a spectacular panelled pinewood ceiling with carved angels and dragons and large gilded chandeliers. The tour ends with the basement kitchens.

Having toured the Schloss, there are some stirring walks to be made in the vicinity. The pathway round the north and west sides

View over the Alps from the summit of Tegelberg

of the building leads up to the **Marienbrücke**, a daringly slender 44m long iron bridge over the **Pöllatschlucht** (Pollat gorge), one regarded as a great technical marvel at the time of its construction in 1866. It offers magnificent views over the truly Wagnerian scenery of the ravine, as well as one of the most familiar picture-postcard panoramas of Neuschwanstein.

Midway along the path between the Schloss and the Marienbrücke, a trail to the left leads down to the floor of the gorge. It passes a plunging waterfall, a renowned local beauty spot, before continuing downwards along the western side of the ravine, alongside the foaming cascades of the stream, and at times along stepped wooden walkways attached to the sides of the rocks. At the Gipsmühle (plaster works), where the Pöllat starts to follow a level course, there is a path leading back in about 10 minutes to the centre of Hohenschwangau.

The overwhelming majority of visitors venture no higher than the Marienbrücke, but the more adventurous follow the marked path up to the summit of **Tegelberg** (1720m), a solid 3 hours' walk away. This at first ascends by means of a seemingly endless series of switchbacks. After about an hour, the most famous of all the views of Neuschwanstein comes into view, in which the castle appears head-on from above, etched against the background of the Alpsee, the Schwansee, the Ammergebirge and the Tyrolean Alps.

The path continues via an exhilarating range of Alpine scenery to the top of the mountain, a particular favourite with balloonists and hang gliding enthusiasts, which itself stands in the lee of the far more formidable Branderschroften (1881m). It can also be reached by the Tegelbergbahn, a cable car whose valley station is a 15 minute walk north of the Gipsmühle. A whole series of wonderful Alpine hikes, embracing all grades of difficulties from straightforward walks to challenging rock climbs, can be made from the Tegelberg summit.

Back down in Hohenschwangau, the official Romantic Road route takes the form of a track along the east side of Schwangauer Strasse, travelling through lush open meadows used for the grazing of cattle. After 1km Schloss Bulbachberg, a large private mansion, can be seen to the left. Immediately beyond, the road changes name to Schloss Strasse, which leads in a further 1km to **SCHWANGAU**, entering the built-up part of the village at the Kurverwaltung building, which stands slightly back from the B17.

Schwangau

Schwangau successfully combines the functions of holiday resort and working agricultural community, and is probably the most convenient base for an extended stay in the area. There is a wide choice of accommodation, and the establishments along the B17 (here known as Füssener Strasse and Münchener Strasse) have the bonus of sweeping vistas across the fields to the royal castles.

Most of Schwangau lies west of the main road. A peculiarity of many of the houses is the presence of a Schupfe, an open lobby with a long wooden bench, where the occupants like to sit on warm summer evenings. This feature was imported from the Engadin region of Switzerland, and is not found in other Allgäu villages. At the western edge of Schwangau is the Kurpark, which commands a view across to the Forggensee. There is a heated open-air swimming pool at its southern edge.

Schwangau's only important historical monument is the much-loved **Wallfahrtskirche St Coloman** (Pilgrimage Church of St Coloman), which lies in splendid isolation in the meadows north of town, reached by a path leading off from the B17. It is by far the best-known of the 39 Bavarian churches dedicated to the saint, an Irish nobleman who was martyred near Vienna, while on his way to Jerusalem, in 1012.

Designed in 1671 by Johann Schmuzer of the prolific Wessobrum School of architects and designers the actual building work was carried out between 1673 and 1685. Outwardly, the architecture is plain and severe, the exception being the octagonal upper storey of the tower, crowned by a characteristic Bavarian onion dome. The interior, however, features a beautiful stuccowork ceiling by Schmuzer himself whilst on the right wall of the nave are charmingly folksy statues of St Coloman, the Virgin Mary and St Apollonia, carved around 1510 by Hans Kels. In honour of his status as the patron saint of livestock, Coloman is depicted as a herdsman in the high altar painting.

The saint's day, which falls on 13th October, is marked by the Colomansfest, whose highpoint comes on the second Sunday of the month with what is undoubtedly, thanks in no small part to the majestic backdrop, one of Germany's most moving and picturesque religious festivals.

STAGE 2:
SCHWANGAU TO STEINGADEN (26km)
(See map p36)

The stretch of the Romantic Road from Schwangau to the next main staging-post of Steingaden is among the most rewarding parts of the route for walkers, offering clear advantages to the traditional motoring route via the B17 road. It makes for a satisfying day's walk, with the choice of making an overnight stop in either Steingaden itself, or in the tranquil surroundings of the Wieskirche. Cyclists will obviously be able, in the course of a day, to combine this stage with several of the shorter stages which follow.

From the northern end of the built-up part of Schwangau's Münchener Strasse, the route turns left, then immediately right, and quits the village via Allemannenweg, which starts out as a street but then quickly assumes the appearance of a farm track. It runs parallel to the B17, offering views of the church of St Coloman to the right, framed by the thickly wooded foothills of the Ammergebirge in the background. The track then crosses two unassuming streams, immediately before they merge: the latter, surprising as it may seem, is the Pöllat. At this point, take the sharp fork to the right, followed almost immediately by another to the left. From there, the track resumes its parallel course to the B17, bypassing Mühlberg, a hamlet consisting of a few farmsteads.

Beyond, at about 3km out of Schwangau, it reaches the **Bannwaldsee**, a typical pre-Alpine lake. It continues northwards along the side of the B17, some way back from the eastern bank of the lake, which has a campsite and boating marina. Further on, there is a good view of the marshy northern shore of the lake, a breeding ground for many species of waterfowl.

At the far end of the Bannwaldsee, the route starts to diverge westwards from the B17, and follows a course through open fields, in the middle of which is a designated picnic spot. After a further 2km, it reaches the eastern entrance to the village of

Bayerniederhofen, and it is well worth making the short detour to see the Pfarrkirche, a good example of the Baroque parish churches so characteristic of rural Bavaria.

The larger village of Buching, which straddles the B17, can be seen a few hundred metres to the east. It is a well developed holiday resort, albeit little patronized by overseas visitors, its main tourist facility being the chairlift to the summit of Buchberg (1142m), the wooded peak to the south.

About 1km beyond Bayerniederhofen, the route crosses the bridge over the River Halblech, and enters Halblech, another resort village, which is primarily of note for being the starting point of a paved road which runs 12km up the wild, dramatic valley to a mountain refuge, the Kenzenhütte (1285m). The Romantic Road route, however, only passes along the fringes of Halblech, taking the first turn left after the bridge, then continuing straight on down to the end of the village.

It then crosses over the road leading north-east to Prem and Lechbruck, then continues on through the fields to Trauchgau, 1km ahead (11km from Schwangau), where it crosses over the B17, which is now left completely behind until Steingaden. Bearing slightly leftwards, it proceeds towards the church, then turns sharp right uphill to the extreme end of the village. Immediately beyond, the route makes a sharp left turn, and begins climbing northwards along a farm road on the brow of the Hoher Traucherg, from where there are fine views over the plateau to the west. After 1km, those in need of a meal or a snack can make a short detour east along the loop trail through a nature reserve and past the site of the Celtic settlement of Hainzenbichl to the Trauchgauer Alm.

A further 1km on, there is a junction. At this point, bear marginally left and cross the Trauchgauer Ach, a mountain stream which forms the northern boundary of Trauchgau, later merging with the Halblech shortly before its confluence with the Lech. The route then ascends a little more steeply than hitherto for a further 1km, before terminating at a T-junction, on either side of which are agricultural hamlets. Immediately to the left is Untschober (or Unter-Schober); the route, however, bears right through Obschober (or Ober-Schober) a few hundred metres ahead. The Allgäu region is now left behind as the route enters the Weilheim-Schongau district of Upper Bavaria

(Oberbayern). This forms part of a larger, albeit rather nebulously defined area which is popularly known as the Pfaffenwinkel (literally, "Clerics' Corner") because of its profusion of churches.

The route continues onwards for 2.5km along a minor road which has the misleadingly grand title of Königstrasse (King Street), descending gently through fields, which give way to woods. There is then a sharp turn leftwards to resume a northerly, ascending course through rich farmland. The hamlet of Resle, which is basically a couple of farmsteads, is reached within 1km; a further 1km beyond, the agricultural country is left behind, and the route travels a level though somewhat snaking course through woodland for 2km, before suddenly descending into a meadow, to the east of which is the Klaperfilz nature reserve, a marshy forest.

Straight ahead, a total of 21km from Schwangau, is the **Wieskirche** (literally, "Meadow Church"), one of the two monuments along the Romantic Road included on UNESCO's highly prestigious World Heritage List. *It is among the supreme creations of the light and airy Rococo style, whose key tenet is the fusion of architecture, painting and decoration into one indivisible whole. The church's matchless sense of unity is a direct result of the relatively short construction period, which lasted from 1746 to 1754, and the close collaboration between the architect Dominikus Zimmermann and his elder brother, the decorative painter Johann Baptist Zimmermann. Both were also stuccoists, and their first major co-operative venture, the Wallfahrtskirche (Pilgrimage Church) at Steinhausen in Upper Swabia, is generally considered Germany's first true Rococo building.*

That such a magnificent building can be found in this isolated spot is due to a complex series of events. In 1730, a Good Friday procession was instigated in Steingaden, for which two of the monks made a wooden figure of the Scourged Christ, reusing limbs from several discarded statues. They draped these in linen, and added a liberal application of red paint to show the wounds. For three years, this served as the focal point of the processions, but it was then withdrawn, on the grounds of being too upsetting, and stored in the attic of the monastery's innkeeper. In 1738, he gave it to his cousin Maria Lori, the wife of a farmer. Shortly afterwards, while praying before it one evening, she noticed that the figure was shedding tears. A tiny chapel was built to house the miraculous statue in 1740, and pilgrims flocked to visit, coming from as far afield as Russia and Spain. Three years later, the Steingaden abbot decided to commission Dominikus Zimmermann to draw up plans for a church large enough to accommodate the volume of visitors.

He chose a strikingly geometric design, consisting of a semi-circular porch, an oval nave (a shape particularly suitable for a pilgrimage church, with its emphasis on processions) and a rectangular choir crowned by a clock tower. The nave is not vaulted, but rather covered with an almost flat wooden ceiling suspened from the roof. By using such a light material the architect was able to employ slender paired columns to covers the vast space, which measures 28m by 18m, and to have two tiers of windows, which flood the gleaming white walls with light.

Johann Baptist Zimmermann's bravura ceiling fresco, executed in glowing pastel-like colours, paints a radiant vision of heaven. In the centre, surrounded by angels and saints, is the Resurrected Christ seated on a rainbow, symbolizing the Convent between God and mankind. At one is the still unoccupied Throne of Judgement, at the other the as yet unopened Gate to Eternity. the small ceiling paintings in the side aisles are mostly devoted to Jesus' ministry of healing, while the eight monochrome pictures set in cartouches above the pillars depict the Beatitudes.

Furnishings in the nave include four large statues of the Doctors of the Church (SS Jerome, Ambrose, Augustine and Gregory) by Anton Sturm, two side altars and four oak confessionals, each with a painting of one of Jesus' parables. At the far end, the riotously ornate pulpit, whose swirling forms symbolize Pentecostal winds, is balanced by the abbot's loft directly opposite.

The focal point of the chancel is the miraculous statue, set in a shrine which is deliberately placed away from the direct light of the windows. It's theme of self-sacrifice is continued in the symbolic carvings of the pelican directly above, and of the lamb surmounting the high altar painting of "The Adoration of the Infant Jesus" by Balthasser Albrecht. Symbolism is also present in the colour scheme of the imitation marble pillars: red represents the shed blood of Chirst, blue God's grace and forgiveness.

Also in the chancel are six vivacious sculptures, of the Evangelists accompanied by the Old Testament prophets Isaiah and Malachi, by Ägidius Verhelst. On the main ceiling fresco by J.B. Zimmermann, god the Father is depicted with angels carring the instruments associated with the Passion. Christ's miracles and teaching are illustrated on the frescoes over the ambulatories, which contain a small selection of the votive offerings left

47

by pilgrims down the centuries.

Immediately to the rear of the Wieskirche is a horseshoe-shaped mansion, originally the summer residence of the Steingaden abbots, and currently used by the ecclesiastical administration. Also by Dominikus Zimmermann is the house immediately north of the church, which he built as his own home. A deeply pious man, he opted to spend his retirement beside his greatest masterpiece (and beside his son, who married the widowed Maria Lori) and lived there until his death in 1766. Nowadays, it is the Café-Gasthof Schweiger, which specializes in excellent and reasonably priced Bavarian cuisine.

*At the foot of the hillock is the simple **Feldkappelle** (Field Chapel), the Wieskirche's immediate predecessor. The parking area beyond is predictably commercialized: over a million visitors come every year, though nowadays a large percentage are artistic rather than religious pilgrims. In order to sample the peaceful rural atmosphere which descends after the church closes (usually around 6pm), it is well worth considering an overnight stop. Accommodation is available in one small inn, and in two of the handful of farmhouses which constitute the hamlet of **WIES**.*

The Romantic Road leads northwards for some 800m to a junction of three roads. On the way, make sure to look back for what are arguably the most imposing views of the Wieskirche, showing the church, as Zimmermann intended, in an almost umbilical relationship with the distant Alpine skyline. At the junction, turn sharp left down a very minor paved road, which leads through farmland, skirting woods and marshes. After 2km, it passes through the tiny hamlet of Litzau, then descends gently for a further 2km to arrive at the southern end of **STEINGADEN**. It is then just a short walk north along the B17 road, here doubling as Füssener Strasse, to the corner of Marktplatz.

STEINGADEN

Rearing above the eastern edge of the square is the little town's overwhelmingly dominant monument, a church which is nowadays usually known as the **Welfenmünster** (Welf Minster). This was originally part of a Premonstratensian monastery, founded in 1147 under the patronage of Duke Welf VI of the eponymous dynasty, the ancestors of the present British royal family. Following secularization in 1803, the church was transferred to parish use, and the monastic buildings demolished, save for one wing of the cloister and the tiny round Johanniskapelle (St John's Chapel) beside the entrance to the enclosure.

The Welfenmünster is of special interest for illustrating virtually the entire history of Bavarian ecclesiastical architecture, changes in taste and desecrations in war having necessitated constant rebuilding. The twin towers, with their steeply pitched saddleback roofs, the groundplan and much of the fabric date from the original Romanesque building period, which ended in 1176. Substantial alterations in Gothic style were made between 1470 and 1491; these include the frescoed Brunnenkapelle (lavabo) in the cloisters and the vaulted entrance porch, which was adorned a century later with a painted genealogy of the Welfs. The Renaissance choir stalls were carved in 1534; the rest of the chancel was redecorated in the 1660s with heavy late Mannerist stuccowork and a new high altar.

To mark the 600th anniversary of the monastery, a masterly Rococo transformation of the nave was carried out between 1740 and 1751. The highly refined stuccowork was executed by Franz Xaver Schmuzer (a grandson of the architect of the Wallfahrtskirche St Coloman), while the showy pulpit was carved by Anton Sturm. Theatricality is also the hallmark of the ceiling frescoes by the Augsburg academician Johann Georg Bergmüller, which illustrate scenes from the life of St Norbert of Xanten, founder of the Premonstratensian Order.

In the scene at the far end, the saint has a vision of the Crucified Christ, while one angel presents him with a plan of the Steingaden monastery and another digs the foundations. The actual building is carried out under the supervision of Duke Welf VI in the scene above the organ, which features an accurate view of how the complex originally looked. In the central fresco, St Norbert appears amid the glory of heaven. His martyrdom is depicted in the small fresco under the tribune, which is flanked by imaginary portraits of Dukes Welf VI and VII.

In moving onwards from Steingaden, cyclists and walkers are faced with a dilemma. Because of the present lack of suitable tracks along the next part of the long-established route of the Romantic Road, the officially designated cycling and walking route currently cuts out two of the traditional staging-posts, Wildsteig and Rottenbuch, and instead follows a direct 14km long course to Peiting, the next stop beyond, travelling along little-used farm roads west of the B17.

It leaves Steingaden via Riesner Strasse, which branches north-westwards from Schongauer Strasse, the northern continuation of Füssener Strasse. Traversing a pastoral landscape of fields and woods, it passes along the western shore of a sausage-shaped lake, the Deutensee, then skirts the eastern bank of the much smaller Riesener See, the approximate halfway point. From there it continues via the hamlets of Stiegl and Geisenberger to Kreut, the only settlement along the stretch which comes near to being a village, and finally bears north-eastwards for the remaining 4km to Peiting.

Other than time-saving, this route has little to recommend it, and it is far better to improvise an alternative passage along the traditional route. This will add, on average, an extra 6km to the distance to be covered, amounting to a total of about 20km from Steingaden to Peiting.

For the first stage, from Steingaden to Wildsteig, there is a choice of three different routes. The shortest of these is the 6km long route along the main road. This initially goes by the name of Ammergauer Strasse, and branches off the B17 a block north of Marktplatz. However, it is preferable to follow Kissingerstrasse eastwards from the Welfenmünster and join the road at the eastern end of Steingaden. Normally, the volume of traffic is tolerably light, and walkers can make use of the ample grassy embankments. The scenery is pleasant enough: the road passes along the Aubach valley, which is sandwiched between two forests - the Schwarzenbacher Wald to

STAGES 3, 4, 5, 6 & 7

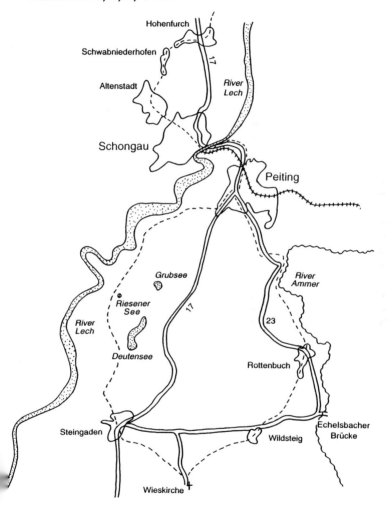

the south and the Ilberger Wald to the north.

The second possibility is to double back to the junction 1km north of the Wieskirche, continuing a short distance eastwards to a college building, the Landvolkshochschule. At this point, walkers can choose between the latter half of the hiking trail described below, or keeping to the cycle route, which loops round to the hamlet of Schwarzenbach 1km on. There it turns right, then left, crosses the Ilach, then goes up the slope, bearing sharp right while still ascending, and arriving at the twin hamlets of Holz and Unterhäusern, 1km before Wildsteig. These two communities share the Dreifaltigkeitskapelle (Holy Trinity Chapel) at the left-hand side of the road. Both inside and out, this looks like a typical little Rococo church, but is actually a skilful pastiche, erected as recently as 1969-70.

The final option, available to walkers but not to cyclists, is to follow the relevant section of the Prälatenweg or "Prelates' Way", a 140km long footpath across the Pfaffenwinkel, linking Marktoberdorf with Kochel am See. This route, which is clearly waymarked with signs showing a clerical staff and the letter P, can be picked up immediately south of Steingaden by following Füssener Strasse to the edge of the village, then turning left into Schlogmühlestrasse and along the valley of the Lumper. It follows a forest path, traverses a meadow, crosses the bridge over the stream, and continues straight ahead through the wet woodland known as the Eulenwald ("Owls' Forest"). At the highest point of this, go slightly right to a convergence of forest trails, and turn leftwards, arriving at a mossy mire, where conditions underfoot are ameliorated by the presence of boards. It is then a short distance through a meadow to the car park on the north side of the Wieskirche.

At this point, the Prelates' Way converges for a time with a much better-known trail, the 120km long König-Ludwig-Weg or King Ludwig Way from Füssen to Starnberg. The latter, which in its early stages occasionally duplicates with the Romantic Road, is marked with signs bearing a large K and a small crown. (See F. and C. Speakman, *King Ludwig Way* [Cicerone].)

From the car park, the combined trail turns northwards, and follows a narrow course alongside a stately avenue of ashes and oaks to the aforementioned Landvolkshochschule. Having passed

Wildsteig, the Leonhardiritt

in front of this, it turns left into a forest path, which goes through the Schwarzenbacher Wald close to the course of the Schwarzenbach stream, though the latter is often obscured by trees. At the junction of paths, it turns right and away from the valley, following a zigzag route through the woodland, before descending again to cross a marshy meadow covered with primroses and orchids in late spring and early summer. At the end of this, the trail joins the road mentioned in the description of the second route, as it climbs towards Holz and Unterhäusern.

WILDSTEIG

A scattered little community set in a typical post-glacial landscape with heath, meadows and pockets of woodland, with a distant view of the Alps, is the most unassuming of all the 26 designated staging-posts along the Romantic Road. Farming remains of far greater significance to the local economy than tourism, as is evident from the ubiquitous presence of grazing livestock in the pastures all around.

The village has one notable monument in the Rococo **Pfarrkirche**

St Jakob (Parish Church of St James), which was built during the last quarter of the 18th century. Outwardly, it is extremely plain, though it does have a tower crowned with a characteristic onion-domed steeple. Inside, there are ceiling paintings by Franz Zwinck, who is best known for his Lüftlmalerei compositions in his native village of Oberammergau. To the rear of the church is a multi-tiered Lourdes Grotto, dating from 1907.

STAGE 4:
WILDSTEIG TO ROTTENBUCH (4km)
(See map p51)

The short journey between Wildsteig and the next staging-post of Rottenbuch can be made via a stretch of the combined Prelates' Way and King Ludwig Way which is suitable for cyclists as well as walkers.

From the Pfarrkirche, it descends northwards to the main road from Steingaden in the valley directly below, crosses over via the tunnel, and proceeds eastwards along the track on the opposite side. After about 1km, it branches to the left away from the main road. The latter continues eastwards for a further 2km to the Echelsbacher Brücke, a spectacular reinforced concrete bridge, completed in 1929, which spans the 76m deep gorge over the River Ammer.

Soon after turning away from the road, the path offers an excellent vantage point, with a sweeping view over the pre-Alpine landscape of the Pfaffenwinkel to the mountains on the horizon. In the foreground is a depression containing the Schwaigsee, a pretty blue lake. A short distance beyond, there is a junction of trails, but the route continues straight ahead, through woods and pastures, before descending the Solder hill. It then arrives at the chalets in the outskirts of **ROTTENBUCH**, and descends to Postplatz, from where an underpass crosses the main road and enters the historic part of the village.

Rottenbuch
This is centred on the former **Klosterstiftskirche** (Monastic Collegiate Church), which has been in parish use since the secularization of 1803. A monastery was first established on the site in the 10th century; in 1073, under the patronage of Duke Welf IV, this was taken over by a congregation of Canons regular of the Augustinian order. The original Romanesque church completed in 1125 was Gothicized in the 1470s, four decades after the addition of the tower, which occupies an unorthodox position jutting out from

the facade.

Save for the porch added in 1777 and the graceful cupola placed above the tower in 1780-1, the exterior is essentially that which can be seen today. The inside, on the other hand, was completely remodelled between 1737 and 1758 and is not only a masterpiece of Rococo interior design of the highest rank, but also a remarkably sensitive treatment of the old fabric, whose original Gothic appearance is still very evident. Particularly outstanding are the frescoes by Matthäus Günther, which illustrate the life of St Augustine.

Only part of the monastery adjoining the church survived the secularization, and only one of the eight outlying chapels escaped demolition. The survivor, the octagonal Frauenbrunnerl (Chapel of the Fountain of Our Lady), nestles by the road leading eastwards out of town, about halfway downhill to the River Ammer. Built in 1688 over a miracle-working spring, it is unostentatious in overall appearance, though its onion-domed central tower has an exotic, slightly Slavic flavour. It is well worth continuing down to the bridge, which offers a pleasant riverside view.

STAGE 5:

ROTTENBUCH TO PEITING (9km)

(See map p51)

For the journey between Rottenbuch and Peiting, cyclists have little option but to stick to the course of the B23. Unfortunately, it is at times necessary to cycle on the road itself, which sometimes has a fair amount of traffic, though in the later stages there is a cycle- and footpath running alongside. Walkers, on the other hand, have the opportunity of following one of the most outstanding stretches of the King Ludwig Way, which parts company with the Prelates' Way at Rottenbuch.

It leaves the village by the gateway just to the north of the Klosterstiftskirche, passes between two fish ponds, then proceeds through meadows at the side of the woods, predominantly of beeches, but also with ashes and alders, high above the Ammer, which is out of sight to the right. At the vantage point of Schweinberg (literally, "Pig Hill"), look backwards for a fine view towards the Alps. Cyclists can negotiate this path, if not always with comfort, for a further 1.5km, but as it enters the woods at the commencement of its steepish descent towards the Ammer, a sign warns that it is thereafter for walkers only.

Although the path ahead could not be called challenging or difficult, some caution is necessary, as it can be wet and muddy in places, and has a few exposed sections. It fords the tiny Talbach (whose name simply means "valley stream"), and continues ahead to the main riverbank, immediately offering a view over one of the most beautiful stretches of the narrow, wild and unspoiled **Ammerleite** (Ammer Canyon). Ahead, an S-bend in the river's course can be seen, and the path gradually moves away from the water's edge and starts to ascend among the trees, though still offering occasional long views.

The King Ludwig Way continues onwards through this marvellous landscape. However, for those following the Romantic Road, it is best to leave the canyon by the first marked path to the left, which leads uphill through the woods and a clearing to the B23. It is then necessary to walk on the road for the best part of 1km, but then a continuous cycle- and footpath can be picked up on the left-hand side, below the chairlift to Strausberg (819m). This continues through the hamlet of Ramsau, then crosses over to the other side of the B23 at the underpass below the highway intersection. Soon afterwards, it arrives in the outskirts of **PEITING**. The town centre is reached by following Bahnhofstrasse and Freistrasse straight ahead, then turning left into Bachstrasse, which leads to Hauptplatz.

Peiting

Nowadays a modest market town of 11,000 inhabitants, Peiting was a place of some importance in the early Middle Ages. It was first documented in 1055 as the site of a castle of Duke Welf I, was later taken over by the imperial Hohenstaufen dynasty, before passing to the Wittelsbach dynasty of Bavarian dukes. Peiting was granted market rights in 1438, and in recognition of the continued importance of this function generally uses the word "Markt" as a prefix to its name.

The route from Rottenbuch enters the town at the southern end of a long, straight road named Untereggstrasse, which terminates at the **Wallfahrtskirche Maria unter den Egg** (literally, "Pilgrimage Church of St Mary under the Corner", the last word being a reference to the location at the edge of a moraine). This modest little church, on which three generations of the Schmuzer family worked, was erected between 1650 and 1665 and partially rebuilt in 1737, though the tower, a skilful pastiche, only dates from 1876. Inside, the Baroque altars, pulpit and Crucifixion group are contemporary with the first building period, the stuccowork with the second.

However, the two most notable furnishings pre-date the church and were brought from elsewhere. Of these, the polychromed wood relief of the Adoration of the Magi in the choir was carved around 1480, while the intriguing painting of the Brotherhood of St James on the west wall is from the early 16th century. The latter, a valuable documentary reference, relates the story of a father and son on a pilgrimage to the saint's shrine. A villainous innkeeper falsely accused them of theft and had them condemned to death by hanging, but the saint miraculously interceded and the culprit was brought to justice and hanged in their place.

Dominating the square is the **Pfarrkirche St Michael** (Parish Church of St Michael), which is 11th century in origin, though only the lower part of the tower and the Communion table inside survive from this period. The crypt (which was formerly an ossuary) and the font both date from the 1330s; the main body of the building was replaced from 1732-5, and is remarkably plain, both inside and out. It does, however, contain three fine altars carved by Franz Xaver Schmädl for Rottenbuch, which were transferred soon after the monastery's suppression.

STAGE 6:
PEITING TO SCHONGAU (4km)
(See map p51)

From the northern end of Peiting's Hauptplatz, the Romantic Road turns right into Schongauer Strasse, which doubles as the stretch of the B17. Beyond the built-up area, there is a cycle- and footpath running all the way alongside the road. The route passes the wooded heights of the Kalvarienberg and Schlossberg to the left, traverses the railway line, then meets up once again with the River Lech.

It arrives in **SCHONGAU** at the train station, the terminus of a branch line from Weilhim via Peiting. From there, the signs point left for the steepish ascent which is the quickest route up to the hilltop town centre.

Schongau

Schongau was established in this location at the turn of the 13th century, moving from a site 3km to the north, which subsequently developed as a separate village named Altenstadt. It gained civic rights in 1331 from Emperor Ludwig the Bavarian, and duly prospered as a trading community. Since the 19th century, it has been an industrial centre, with paper, electrical appliances, dairy products, woollens and electricity generation the most important activities. As a corollary, it has expanded its area considerably, stretching well over the valley below.

Nonetheless, the upper part of Schongau is still encircled by the **Stadtmauer** (Town Wall), which survives virtually intact, with most of the structure seemingly pre-dating the fire of 1493 which ravaged the town. Parts of the wall were sold off to local residents in the early 19th century, and remain in private hands. However, the outer side of the entire circuit has been laid out as a shady public promenade, and it is well worth walking all the way round it.

The area around the south-east corner tower, the **Kasslturm**, is now a war memorial. Proceeding westwards, the southern entrance

Schongau, the sentry walk of the Stadtmauer

to the town is guarded by the **Polizeidienerturm** ("Police Servant Tower"), which at 17.5m is the highest of the towers, one commanding a view towards the Alps. Continuing in a clockwise direction, the next landmark is the **Frauentor** (Lady Gate), the western gateway to the town. This takes its name from the statue of the Virgin Mary above its archway, which was carved by the sculptor and mayor Johann Pöllandt in 1700.

Further north, the strongest part of the fortifications protected the **Schloss**, a secondary residence of the Wittlesbach dukes which is nowadays the offices of the local district administration. It has been shorn of its defensive features in the many transformations it has undergone down the centuries, though the Maxtor, the former court gate, still survives.

A path leads down from there to the one significant monument outside the walls, the **Heiligkreuzkapelle** (Holy Cross Chapel), a miniature pilgrimage church built by Johann Schmuzer from 1690-3 and extended by his son Joseph in 1725. At the high altar is a Crucifixion group by Johann Pöllandt.

Curiously, the eastern section of the wall always lacked towers.

This was presumably due to its being the least prone to attack, partly because it commands the steepest slope, and partly because it overlooked friendly Bavarian territory only. It preserves an intact section of the **Wehrgang** (sentry walk), and at least part of this is always freely accessible.

The most convenient point of access is from the grounds of the **Heilig-Geist-Spital** (Holy Ghost Hospital) on Karmelitergasse, which lies immediately to the left when entering the town walls on the route up from the station via the signposted Romantic Road route. Nowadays an old folks' home, the hospice was, until the Napoleonic secularization, a monastery of the Discalced Carmelites.

The adjoining **Heilig-Geist-Kirche** (Holy Ghost Church) was begun in 1720, the year after the order arrived in Schongau, and completed in 5 years. Joseph Schmuzer was the executant architect, but the sober Baroque architecture is untypical of the Wessobrunn style, instead reflecting the ascetic ideals of the monks who commissioned it. It does, however, contain some fine furnishings, notably the pulpit donated by the wealthy Sepp family and the high altar with a painting by Gottfried Bernhard Göz depicting the Holy Trinity and the Virgin Mary with her parents.

Altogether more sumptuous is Schongau's other main church, the **Stadtpfarrkirche Mariä Himmelfahrt** (Town Parish Church of the Assumption), which lies a block to the north on the central square, Marienplatz. The tower and chancel were built immediately after their Gothic predecessors collapsed in 1667. In 1748, Dominikus Zimmermann decorated the interior of the latter with a scheme of exquisite grey, rose and gold stuccowork, and drew up plans for a new nave, which was built in 1751-3.

Closing the southern side of Marienplatz is the step-gabled **Ballenhaus** (Ball House), which was built in 1419 and extended in 1515. It served a variety of functions, and the richly decorated Ratsstube (Council Chamber) on the first floor was for long the seat of the local government administration. In 1902, it was superseded in this role by the Baroque palace opposite its western elevation, which has fine stuccowork by Franz Schmuzer. Although generally known as the **Altes Rathaus** (Old Town Hall), it only served as such until 1926, when it was replaced by a new building immediately north of the Stadtpfarrkirche, and now serves as a music school.

On the eastern side of the square, the most notable building is the **Finanzamt** (Finance Office), which is directly opposite the fountain. It was built in the late 17th century as the revenue office of the monastery of Rottenbuch, and remodelled in 1810 to serve the same function on behalf of the new Kingdom of Bavaria. On the opposite side of the fountain is Löwenstrasse, on which stands the former **Stadtapotheke** (Town Pharmacy), with its charming inner courtyard.

At this end of this street, Christophstrasse leads north to the **Stadtmuseum** (Town Museum). This occupies the deconsecrated 14th century church of the original Heilig-Geist-Spital, which was decorated with white stuccowork by Johann Pöllandt. It contains displays of archaeological finds, local history, art and folklore, and a valuable collection of coins from Celtic times to the present day, many from a recently discovered medieval hoard.

At Schongau, the Romantic Road route for walkers and cyclists deviates altogether from the traditional motoring route along the B17. Rather than follow the direct 4km road to the next staging-post of Hohenfurch - the only point of convergence between the two routes until Landsberg am Lech - it leaves the town via Altenstädter Strasse, the road leading north-west from the junction immediately below the Heiligkreuzkapelle. This follows a snaking 2km long uphill course to ALTENSTADT (a corruption of Alte Stadt, or "Old Town"), the village which grew up on the original site of Schongau, after the latter had moved to its present site.

Even from afar, the monumental 32m high twin towers of the church of **St Michael** can be seen. *This is the only vaulted Romanesque basilica to have survived in the whole of Upper Bavaria, and its clean, pure architectural lines make a refreshing antidote to the relentless colour and decorative profusion of almost all the other major churches in the province. Constructed of tufa ashlars, it was built some time between 1180 and 1220, and displays the clear influence of the architecture of the Italian province of Lombardy. Entry is through the deeply recessed facade portal, whose carved tympanum depicts a knight defeating a winged dragon.*

The focal point of the interior is the great Triumphal cross. An equally precious example of Romanesque carving is the stone font in the northern aisle, whose basin has reliefs of St Michael Trampling Lucifer, St John the Baptist in the Wilderness, the Baptism of Christ and the Enthroned Madonna and Child.

From the church, it is perhaps easiest to continue all the way through Altenstadt via the main road, which follows the course of the Schönach, a Lech tributary which rises outside Schwabsoien, the next village to the west. However, to follow the official marked route, it is necessary to double back towards Schongau, and to take the penultimate street to the left. This leads out of the village

Landsberg am Lech, the Ruethenfest

Augsburg, view from the Perlachturm, looking south
Nördlingen, the sentry walk of the Stadtmauer

northwards along a path laid out along the route of a Roman road, the Via Claudia Augusta. It meets up with the main road in Schwabniederhofen, 1.5km on, passes all the way through the middle of the village, then crosses the tracks of the Schongau to Landsberg railway line, which is now used for goods services only.

Immediately beyond lies **HOHENFURCH**, an elongated village spread out along both sides of the Schönach.

Hohenfurch

Essentially a farming community, with tourism no more than a sideline, it rivals Wildsteig as the most low-key of all the official staging-posts along the Romantic Road. Until 1802, it was two separate villages, Oberhohenfurch and Unterhohenfurch, which had different feudal allegiances. The B17 road, which splices the village vertically in exactly the same place as the traditional boundary, ensures that the sense of duality remains.

There are two notable historic monuments at the far end of Unterhohenfurch, the part lying east of the B17. The **Pfarrkirche Mariä Himmelfahrt** (Parish Church of the Assumption) preserves a 14th century tower with a 15th century bell chamber and saddle roof, but was otherwise completely rebuilt between 1738 and 1750. Although far less sumptuous than any of the great monastic, pilgrimage or civic churches of the period, it is nonetheless an unusually rich example of parochial Bavarian Rococo.

The best view of Hohenfurch is that from a hillock beyond the built-up part of the village, just a few hundred metres south-east of the Pfarrkirche, on which stands the late Gothic chapel of **St Ursula**. Built in 1520, it has a turret and entrance porch to enliven its otherwise plain exterior, which eccentrically omits windows on the west and north sides. Sadly, it has long lain completely neglected, a sitting target for vandals and thieves, who have duly spirited away the valuable sculptures from its original altarpiece.

Except for the last few kilometres, this stage lies almost entirely along very minor country roads on which there is currently only the occasional special track for walkers and cyclists. However, the volume of traffic is extremely low, and this is a particularly rewarding part of the journey, taking in some fine scenery as well as a couple of little-known but fascinating villages which are not part of the traditional motoring route.

The signposted way out of Hohenfurch lies midway between the B17 and the Pfarrkirche, though the road northwards from beside the church can be taken as an alternative, as the two shortly afterwards join up. It is some 4km through pastoral countryside to Kinsau, which lies slightly back from a point where the Lech briefly separates into two channels. The main part of the village, which lies down in the valley, is bypassed by the Romantic Road, which continues onwards along the side of the woods which lie steeply above the Lech. After about 2km, a grandstand view of the river can be glimpsed through the trees.

Another 2km on, the road makes a sharp turn down to **EPFACH**, which occupies a picturesque situation on an S-bend of the Lech. *As the successor to the Roman settlement of Abodiacum, this can claim to rank among the oldest villages in Germany, though the site is not absolutely identical. The former fire station building on the main street, Hauptstrasse, has recently been converted to house the* **Museum Abodiacum***. This contains a model of the Roman town, plus coins, terracottas, pottery and sculptural fragments found during excavations. There is also a statue of its most celebrated son, Claudius Paternus Clementianus, whose distinguished Imperial career culminated in a spell as a successor in Pontius Pilate's role as Governor of Judea, after which he retired to his native town in AD 125.*

Immediately beyond the present-day village, just before the bridge over the Lech, a path leads uphill to the Baroque **St-Lorenz-Kapelle** (St Lawrence's Chapel), the sole building on the site of Abodiacum. Once over the river, the route climbs quite steeply;

indeed, this is one of the few noticeable inclines along the entire Romantic Road, rising nearly 90m in altitude in the 2km to Reichling, which is at the highest elevation of any place since Rottenbuch. The first 1km of this is wooded, but thereafter there are sweeping views over the Lech valley. Look out also for a fine example of a wayside shrine in a field to the left.

Beyond Reichling, a village with a handsome Baroque Pfarrkirche, the road begins a very gradual but pronounced descent all the way to Landsberg. After travelling 3km through farming country it reaches **VILGERTSHOFEN**, whose **Wallfahrtskirche Mariä Himmelfahrt** (Pilgrimage Church of the Assumption) can be seen from afar. *This was built between 1687 and 1692 by Johann Schmuzer, though embellishments continued to be made until the middle of the following century, adding Rococo touches to the original Baroque. It adopts a centralized, Greek-cross plan, but the exterior has a slightly lopsided effect as only one of the two planned towers was built, and that belatedly. Inside, the stuccowork, mostly white on coloured grounds, is a*

STAGE 8

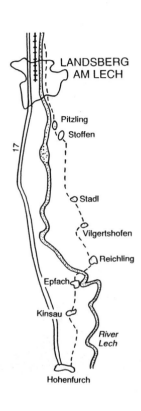

Vilgertshofen, the Wallfahrtskirche Mariä Himmelfahrt

particularly outstanding manifestation of the Wessobrunn style.

The two-tier high altar, by the architect's son Franz I, incorporates the miraculous 15th century Pietà group which is the goal of the pilgrimages. These culminate each year in the Sunday after the Feast of the Assumption (15th August), when the Stumme Prozession (Silent Procession) is held. In this, the traditional liturgical parade walks behind costumed groups enacting over a hundred different tableaux of events from the Old and New Testaments.

Leaving Vilgertshofen, the Romantic Road continues through somewhat featureless farming country, passing through the village of Stadl, just over 1km on, and continuing northwards for a further 5km to Stoffen. In the latter part of the route, there is a brief forest interlude as it passes through the eastern abutment of the Schlegelwald, which reaches down to the banks of the Lech. At Stoffen, the route assumes a north-westerly direction, and descends to the centre of Pitzling, 3km on; it travels through the village, at the end of which it finally reaches the Lech. A lovely 3km long forest track through the coniferous Pössinger Wald then hugs the riverbank all the way to Landsberg.

Landsberg am Lech

The site of **LANDSBERG AM LECH** is known to have been inhabited in the Bronze Ages, though its history as a permanent settlement does not begin until the 12th century. Around 1180 the Welf prince Henry the Lion (Heinrich der Löwe), Duke of Bavaria and Saxony, built a fortress known as Landespurc at the crossing-point of the long-established trade route between Augsburg and Northern Italy, and the newer, highly lucrative salt road linking the saline-producing town of Reichenhall with Upper Swabia, an area which was deficient in this commodity. A town quickly grew up between this fortress and the River Lech. It established a strong craft tradition which survived right up until the belated industrialization of the 1870s.

As befits a long-time frontier town - it served as Bavaria's westernmost outpost until the Napoleonic period - Landsberg has had a chequered history. During its prosperous periods, notably in the 15th and 18th centuries, it was able to commission showpiece public buildings which give the townscape a grandeur which belies its modest size: it had just 2000 inhabitants in the mid-18th century, and has 24,000 today.

In the first half of the 20th century, however, it gained notoriety as the site of a jail for high-profile prisoners. Adolf Hitler was interned there following the failure of the 1923 Munich Beer Hall Putsch, and he used the time to dictate to Rudolf Hess the text of *Mein Kampf* (literally, "My Struggle").

Most of the southern, eastern and northern ranges of the **Stadtmauer** (Town Wall) have survived, and a walk round them makes for a good beginning to a tour of the town. The obvious place to begin is at the late 14th century **Nonnenturm** (Nuns' Tower), which takes its name from the nearby convent. It overlooks the Lech and, lying just beyond the edge of the Pössinger Wald, is the first monument encountered by those travelling the Romantic Road by bicycle or on foot. One of the many stairways bridging the town's steep streets leads up to the so-called **Jungfernsprung** ("Virgins' Leap"), a semi-circular tower from the 15th century.

The promenade alongside the wall leads up to the mighty **Bayertor** (Bavarian Gate), the most imposing medieval gateway in Southern Germany and nowadays the symbol of Landsberg. Completed in 1425 as the crowning glory of a complete revamping of the municipal fortifications, it stands at an elevation 40m above that of the lower town. An outer barbican guards a 36m high tower, whose outer face is adorned with a monumental carved scene of the Crucifixion. In the summer months, the tower can be ascended for a view which on clear days reaches as far as the Alps, though for reasons of topography does not embrace all the town's chief landmarks.

From the Bayertor, the promenade continues along the length of the eastern course of the wall to the **Pulverturm** (Powder Tower) in the corresponding position to the north. The path then enters the woods and starts descending, passing the **Dachlturm**, an observation tower which likewise dates from the 15th century, on the way down to the **Sandauer Tor** (Sandau Gate), the northern entrance to the town. The latter was remodelled in 1630, and has a certain Mannerist elegance which sets it apart from the rest of the fortifications. Alongside is the **Staffingerhof**, a picturesque 17th century arcaded courtyard.

A short way down Vorderer Anger, the eastern of the two streets leading into the town centre from the gateway, is the **Johanniskirche** (St John's Church), a miniature Rococo masterpiece built during 1750-2 by Dominikus Zimmermann, who was a longstanding Landsberg resident and sometime mayor prior to his retirement to live beside the Wieskirche. Although he was allocated just 12m on the street front, he nonetheless created a wonderfully rhythmical facade which serves as the perfect prelude to the interior.

A few paces beyond the church, the alley to the right, Hintere Mühlgasse, leads to the 15th century **Bäckertor** (Bakers' Gate), which has a curious dual profile, with a stepped gable on its eastern facade, a hipped roof on the western side. On the other side of the canal is the **Färbertor** (Drapers' Gate) which assumed its present form in the mid-16th century.

Returning to the main axis, which changes name from Vorderer Anger to Ludwigstrasse, the **Stadtpfarrkirche Mariä Himmelfahrt** (Town Parish Church of the Assumption) looms ahead. This was begun in late Gothic style in 1458 under Matthäus Ensinger, a member of a well-known dynasty of masons from Ulm, and completed in 1488. In the late 17th and early 18th centuries, a partial programme of modification in line with the Baroque tastes then current was carried out. This included the heightening of the tower by the addition of an upper storey and bulbous dome, and the substitution of the original rib vaulting with a smooth surface suitable for covering with Wessobrunn stuccowork.

Ludwigstrasse terminates at Landsberg's sloping main square, the triangular-shaped Hauptplatz. At its top end is a brick clock tower which dates back to the time of the earliest municipal defensive system in the late 13th century. It is alternatively known as the **Schöner Turm** ("Beautiful Tower") and the **Schmalzturm** ("Lard Tower"), the latter nickname coming from the product which used to be traded in its passageway. In the centre of Hauptplatz is the **Marienbrunnen** (St Mary's Fountain), which was erected in 1783.

Unusually, the **Rathaus** (Town Hall) is sandwiched among a row of mansions on the northern side of the square. It was built between 1699 and 1702, but the exuberant stuccowork facade, Dominikus Zimmermann's only major secular commission, was not added until 1719. The great architect also decorated the Ratsstube

(Council Chamber) on the second floor, which was later adorned with two huge group paintings by Hubert von Herkomer, who is nowadays a rather neglected figure, but who had an immensely successful career in Victorian England, where he was taken as a child, staying on to establish his own art college. The festive room on the third floor has four large murals by the 19th century painters Ferdinand Piloty and Eduard Schwoiser illustrating key events in the history of Landsberg.

From the gateway in the Schmalzturm, Alte Bergstrasse begins its snaking ascent up to the Bayertor. A short way up, there is a staircase which leads in two stages to a late 17th century building, originally the Jesuit grammar school, which is home to the **Neues Stadtmuseum** (New Town Museum). This has a comprehensive series of displays on local archaeology, history and art, the most valuable treasure being a late Gothic sculptural group of the Coronation of the Virgin.

Immediately opposite is the twin-towered **Heilig-Kreuz-Kirche** (Holy Cross Church), which was built for the Jesuits in 1752-4. Although architecturally rather ordinary, it has a pleasing sense of space, and boasts an excellent illusionistic ceiling fresco by Christoph Thomas Scheffler depicting the Legend of the Cross. On the north side of the church is the **Arkadenhof** ("Arcaded Court"), the former Jesuit college, built at the turn of the 17th century.

Back down on Hauptplatz, Herkomerstrasse leads south past the brightly painted **Klosterkirche** (Convent Church), built in 1765-6 to replace its predecessor, which Dominikus Zimmermann had erected just 40 years earlier. The street then swings round to cross the Lech via the Karolinenbrücke, which commands a fine view of the town's skyline, and of the Lechwehr (Lech Weir) directly to the north.

On the opposite bank, Von-Kühlmann-Strasse leads northwards to the **Mutterturm** (Mother Tower), which was built by Herbert von Herkomer from 1884-8 in honour of his recently widowed mother to serve as his Landsberg studio. Inside is a representative sample of his graphic art. The tower is linked by a covered passageway to the large mansion which was the home of the artists' parents. Now designated the **Herkomer-Museum**, this contains a fine collection of his portrait and landscape paintings and drawings. There is also documentary material on his varied outside interests. As is evidenced by his portraits, he knew many leading figures in the world of music, and was himself an occasional composer. He was also an early enthusiast for automobiles, funding his own racing competition, and was among the first to recognize the importance of film as a new artistic medium.

LANDSBERG AM LECH TO FRIEDBERG (43km)

For this stage through the Lech valley, the cycle and walking route initially travels along the opposite side of the river from the B17 followed by the motoring route; when it does cross over, it still keeps well to the east of the main road. Indeed, on this stretch there is not a single point of convergence between the two routes, which are very different in character.

For much of this stage, the cycle and walking route travels through countryside which, if not exactly wilderness, is often well away from any human habitation. The landscapes are varied and often unexpectedly attractive, though as a result of almost continuous damming the River Lech itself is far less scenic than at almost any other point along its course. One small snag is that Klosterlechfeld, the one and only place of major historical interest in this stage of the motoring route, is bypassed, though it is a straightforward detour of just 3km each way to get there.

Walkers have the larger problem that this stage, even without the recommended detour. It is a fairly demanding day's hike, and there is no obvious place to break for the night: accommodation along the way, and particularly in the latter part, is all but non-existent. However, the absence of setpiece attractions means that it is easy to keep to a fixed timetable; furthermore, there are several possible "escape routes" enabling the journey to be continued by public transport, should the need arise.

The official route leaves Landsberg by Epfenhauser Strasse, which runs alongside the eastern stretch of the Stadtmauer. Once over the A96/E54 road, it passes just east of the village of Sandau, which is nowadays incorporated into the municipality of Landsberg, though it can trace its origins back even earlier, archaeological finds from the 8th century having been discovered there. The track continues through fields, then skirts the woods above the Lech, before terminating at a T-junction. It then turns left, then after 200m turns right to cross the railway tracks and enters Kaufering. Although

STAGES 9 & 10

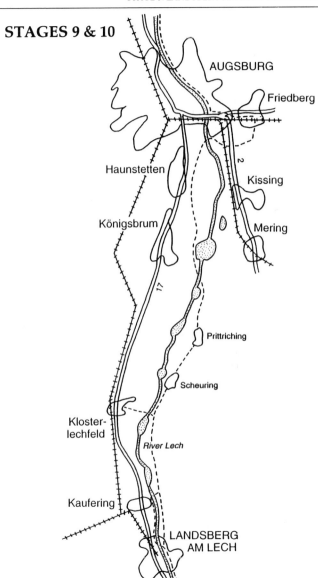

AUGSBURG

Friedberg

Haunstetten

Kissing

Königsbrum

Mering

17

Prittriching

Scheuring

Kloster-
lechfeld

River Lech

Kaufering

LANDSBERG
AM LECH

most of the town, which is 6km from Landsberg, now lies on the other side of the Lech, this is the historic part, dominated by the Baroque Pfarrkirche (Parish Church).

It is worth knowing that there is an alternative, and arguably more scenic way of reaching Kaufering. This leaves Landsberg by the Sandauer Tor, continuing along Sandauer Strasse to cross the Lech by the Sandauer Brücke. Immediately to the right, there is a path, suitable for cyclists as well as walkers, which closely follows the riverside all the way to the bridge linking the two parts of Kaufering. Crossing over to the other side, the Romantic Road signposts can be picked up in the town centre, immediately below the church.

Having travelled northwards all the way through Kaufering, the route continues for about 1.5km beside the trees above the Lech, before entering the Westerholz (literally, "West Wood") along a track parallel to the old Roman road, which still preserves its entrenchments. After another 1km or so it emerges out of the woodland and once again follows a course between the trees above the river and the pastoral land to the east. At the hamlet of Haltenberg it passes close to a ruined castle before arriving at a lodge which is a popular refreshment stop with local ramblers in summer. The path then descends quickly to one of the Lech reservoirs; a short distance beyond, it reaches a road, where it turns left to the Zollhaus restaurant, some 8km from Kaufering.

A few paces to the west is a bridge commanding a pleasant view of the river; a further 3km along the road is **KLOSTERLECHFELD**, which makes for a highly recommended detour. *The village occupies the site of the Battle of Lechfeld of 955, which saw the defeat of the invading Hungarians by Emperor Otto the Great. Its history as a settlement, however, did not begin until 1603, when Regina von Imhof, the widow of a burgomaster of Augsburg, was lost there in a dense fog. She prayed to the Virgin Mary, promising to found a chapel to her if the skies cleared, as they duly did. The municipal architect of Augsburg, Elias Holl, was then commissioned to design a simple rotunda, which took the Pantheon in Rome as its model. Pilgrims soon started flocking to the shrine, and by 1606 Franciscans had arrived to establish a monastery.*

Between 1656-9, Karl Dietz the Younger built the present **Wallfahrtskirche Maria Hilf** *("Pilgrimage Church of Mary's Help"),* *and in the following years the original rotunda was remodelled to serve as its sanctuary. In 1690-1, two smaller round chapels, each likewise crowned with an onion-domed turret, were added to the sides. The interior of the whole church was completely transformed in Rococo style during 1739-48. Both the high altar and the main ceiling fresco illustrate the theme of Christ as Judge, with the Virgin Mary and St Michael as intercessors.*

Between the church and the main square, Marktplatz, is the **Kalvarienberg** *(Calvary). This is centred on another rotunda, above which stands a life-sized group of sculptures depicting the Crucifixion. Two other Stations of the Cross, the Agony in the Garden of Gethsemane and the Entombment of Christ, are housed in the chambers above and below the stairway, while the other 12 are in shrines around the perimeter of the walled garden.*

Returning the 3km to the Zollhaus, the route proceeds northwards for 2km to pass all the way through Scheuring, a small farming community with two Baroque churches. The first of these was built for parish use, whereas its counterpart at the northern exit to the village has its origin in a pilgrimage. Beyond, the track leaves the roadside and goes 2.5km through the fields, finally ending at a T-junction, where it turns right into Prittriching. This has another fine church, Gothic by origin, though later decorated with Wessobrunn stuccowork. The route skirts all along the western fringe of the village, turns sharp left then right, and proceeds through the fields.

Soon after, it leaves Upper Bavaria, and enters the province of Swabia (Schwaben), an area which only became part of Bavaria in 1803 as a result of Napoleon's abolition of a host of city-states and ecclesiastical territories. It is only a small part of the much larger medieval duchy of the same name, which also encompassed most of the modern Land of Baden-Württemberg.

After 3km, the route leaves the fields, swinging leftwards to cross a dam on the Lech. Once over, it makes a switchback to reach the western side of a narrow canal. It follows this northwards, along avenues of dogwoods and through a beautiful nature reserve of heath and mixed forest. It then passes below a large reservoir and continues over a road which offers the most convenient "escape routes" for walkers who are behind schedule: 2km to the west lies Königsbrunn, which is within Augsburg's municipal bus network, while 4km to the east is Mering, which has a station on the Augsburg to Munich railway line.

For the next 9km, the Romantic Road leads through a stretch of thick mixed woodland in which coniferous trees predominate. Though now somewhat seamless, this goes under three different names: the southern section is known as the Stadtwald ("Town Forest"), the middle as the Haunstetter Wald and the northern as the Siebentischwald ("Seven Tables Forest"). Whereas the first two are natural, the last-named is actually an English-style park, laid out in 1873-5 on what was then an open meadow. Its curious name is explained by the fact that a tavern with seven tables was formerly located there. The whole area is criss-crossed with trails, so there is no imperative to follow the signposted route, which travels through the western part of the forest, emerging out of the Haunstetter Wald to skirt through the fields east of Haunstetten, the satellite town sandwiched between Ausburg and Königsbrunn, before cutting a diagonal path through the Siebentischwald.

Both this route, and the obvious alternative - to go continuously through the woods by the path below the Lech - terminate at the Hochablasswehr, a weir first documented as far back as the mid-14th century. The present reinforced concrete dam was erected immediately after the disastrous floods of 1911-12. Alongside is a 660m long canoeing slalom course, which was specially constructed for the 1972 Olympic Games and is still the national headquarters for the sport.

From there, it is only 1km north to the main B300 road which leads westwards for 3km to the centre of Augsburg. However, at this point the official Romantic Road route makes a looping detour to the east. It crosses over the Lech by the dam, then bears right along the eastern shore of the Kuhsee ("Cow Lake"), an artificial stretch of water created in 1970-2 to serve as a summertime sailing and bathing spot.

There it turns leftwards to skirt the extreme southern end of Augsburg's eastern bank suburb of Hochzoll, passing through the tunnel under the Augsburg-Munich railway to emerge at the B2 road linking the same two cities. It turns right, then immediately left, to reach the little village of Metzgerhof and the roadside church of St Afra im Feld (St Afra in the Field), built in 1710 on the supposed site of the martyrdom in 304 of the eponymous saint, a Cypriot princess killed for her refusal to renounce Christianity.

From just in front of the church there is a fine view over the fields to Friedberg. To reach the town, the track initially runs parallel to the road, branching off to the right just before the Baggersee reservoir. It travels along the valley of the Hagenbach through fields and parkland to emerge in the southern outskirts at a street known as Am Fladerlach. This bears right into Hagelmühlweg, at the end of which it turns left down Am Bierweg.

Just before the junction below, it is worth making a short detour to the west to see the little Baroque church of St Stephan, which was built in 1698 as a leper hospital. Back at the junction, the route passes over the concealed railway line and ascends along Münchner Strasse. The second street on the left, Ludwigstrasse, leads to the town centre.

Friedberg

Although its population falls short of 30,000, **FRIEDBERG** is nevertheless the third largest town on the Romantic Road, surpassed only by the great cities of Augsburg and Würzburg. Lying just 7km from the centre of the former, it might appear to be just another satellite town, but its commanding hilltop position gives the lie to this. In fact, Friedberg stood for centuries in an adversarial position to its powerful neighbour. It was founded in 1264 under the joint auspices of Duke Ludwig II and his nephew Conradin, the last member of the Imperial Hohenstaufen dynasty, for the express purpose of providing Bavaria with a bulwark against the ambitions of Augsburg and its Prince-Bishops. Like Landsberg, it served as a Bavarian frontier-post until part of Swabia was allocated to Bavaria as a result of Napoleon's reordering of the map of Germany.

The central Marienplatz, lined with mansions erected by wealthy burghers, is dominated by the **Rathaus** (Town Hall), which was erected in the 1670s, at a time when Friedberg's fortunes had revived in the wake of the conclusion of the Thirty Years' War. Its grand end gables, its onion-domed turret, and even its cornices and door and window frames are all imitations of the architectural vocabulary of the grand late Renaissance public buildings Elias Holl designed in Augsburg at the beginning of the same century. At the south-east corner of the square is the **Marienbrunnen** (St Mary's Fountain). Originally this was a thanksgiving column to the Virgin, commemorating Friedberg's deliverance from the plague in 1599; it was not until 1788 that it was supplied with water.

Running off the north-east corner of Marienplatz is **Uhrmachergasse** ("Clockmakers' Alley"), the traditional home of the families who made Friedberg's most prestigious product. The clockmaking tradition flourished in the town from the mid-17th century to the early 19th century, and still survives to this day. Over 350 local clockmakers are documented, and examples of the beautiful Baroque and Rococo timepieces they created can be seen in museums all over the world. On Jesuitengasse, immediately to the west, is the former **Jesuitenkirche** (Jesuit Church) of 1588, which was converted into a mansion in 1885.

A block west of the Marienbrunnen is the **Stadtkirche St Jakob** (Town Church of St James), whose 56m high belfry is the most prominent feature of Friedberg's skyline, for all that its Italianate form makes it an unusual, not to say incongruous, main landmark for a German medieval town. The Gothic church which formerly occupied the spot was gravely damaged in 1868, when the tower collapsed. Partly on grounds of cost, and partly in line with the artistic tastes then current in the Kingdom of Bavaria, it was decided to replace this with a new building based on the architectural principles of the early Christians. Thus the interior was modelled on the basilica of San Apollinare in Classe outside Ravenna, though it was the great Romanesque church of San Zeno in Verona which provided the inspiration for the exterior.

Inside, the walls are adorned with frescos by the Nazarene artist Ferdinand Wagner. In the southern aisle of the nave is a beautifully carved Gothic memorial tablet in honour of Duke Ludwig the Bearded, who provided Friedberg with a new set of municipal defences between 1409 and 1412.

The western stretch of the **Stadtmauer** (Town Wall) is the only part not dismantled by the French in the Napoleonic Wars. It can be explored via the lane of the same name, which runs along its inner perimeter, past the seven surviving towers. Starting at the south-west corner, these are successively the Wasserturm (Water Tower), the Büchsenmacher Turm (Gunsmiths' Tower), the Zwingerturm

(Bastion Tower), the Näglersturm, the Hagersturm, the Folterturm (Torture Tower) and the Pulverturm (Powder Tower).

Beyond the last-named, at the north-western edge of the defences, is the **Schloss**. Almost nothing remains of the original 13th century fortress, which was rebuilt between 1550 and 1560, and again after the Thirty Years' War. Part of it houses the **Heimatmuseum** (Local Museum), though this is only open for a few hours each week. The vaulted Rittersaal (Knights' Hall), the only important historical interior, contains sacred sculpture. Elsewhere, there are fine collections of locally produced pocket watches, table clocks and carriage clocks, and of the plates, bowls and mugs made in the faience manufactory which operated in the Schloss itself between 1756 and 1768. When the museum is open, it is also possible to ascend the tower for a view over the town.

From the Schloss, Burgwallstrasse and Hermann-Löns-Strasse lead east to the **Wallfahrtskirche Herrgottsruh** (literally, "Pilgrimage Church of the Lord God's Rest"), which was built between 1731 and 1753 by Johann Benedikt Ettl to replace a chapel founded at an uncertain date in the Middle Ages by a Friedberg pilgrim in thanks for his safe passage home, following his imprisonment in a Turkish jail while returning from Jerusalem. The somewhat lumpy appearance of the exterior is in part a consequence of the idiosyncratic design of the interior, which features no fewer than seven domes. It was decorated by several of the leading craftsmen of the day, and ranks among the finest achievements of Bavarian Rococo.

The frescoes of the choir, painted in 1738, are the last work of one of Bavaria's most prolific artists and designers, Cosmos Damian Asam. On the walls, he painted the joint patrons of the church, the Holy Trinity and the Three Magi; the eight unequal compartments of the ceiling together make up a complicated allegory on the theme of Redemption. The other six domes were frescoed by Johann Georg Bergmüller.

STAGE 10:
FRIEDBERG TO AUGSBURG (7km)
(See map p75)

Given that it lies almost entirely through built-up areas - the suburbs of Augsburg stretch just short of the municipal boundary of Friedberg - this short stage is the least eventful of all along the Romantic Road.

From the Wallfahrtkirche Herrgottsruh, the quickest way back to Friedberg's Marienplatz is south-westwards via Herrgottruhstrasse and Ludwigstrasse. Friedberger Berg loops downhill below the Stadtmauer to the B300 road, which has a cycle and walking track along its northern side; this leads through the suburb of Friedberg-West to Hochzoll.

On reaching the River Lech, there is a choice of routes into the centre of Augsburg. Continuing straight ahead over the bridge, Friedberger Strasse goes all the way to the Heilig-Geist-Spital in the southern part of the city's historic core. Alternatively, follow the Romantic Road signs down into the park on the eastern bank and on to the track which leads northwards along the riverside all the way through the city. Crossing over the next bridge, the Lechhäuser Brücke, follow Lechhäuser Strasse, which bears right into Jaboberstrasse. Two small streets, Barfüsserstrasse and Perlachberg, then lead directly from there to the main square, Rathausplatz.

Augsburg
With a population of around a quarter of a million, **AUGSBURG** is by far the largest, as well as the oldest, city along the course of the Romantic Road. Its name, which means "Fortress of Augustus", is a direct translation of that of the original Roman settlement of Augusta Vindelicorum, which was founded in 15BC by Drusus and Tiberius, the stepsons of Augustus Caesar.

Although its history during the Dark Ages is somewhat obscure, Augsburg had become the seat of a bishopric by the 9th century, perhaps as a result of the popularity of the cult of St Afra. In the

Augsburg, the Herkulesbrunnen and the Schaezler-Palais

following century, the redoubtable Bishop (later St) Ulrich fortified the city, which resisted the invading Magyars prior to their final defeat at the Battle of Lechfeld.

Augsburg was first chartered in 1156, and was regularly chosen for meetings of the Imperial Diet. It became a Free Imperial City in 1276, thus gaining independence from the local Prince-bishops, who continued to govern the surrounding area. In the 15th and 16th centuries, the Fugger and Welser dynasties made it Europe's most important centre of high finance. Jakob Fugger "The Rich" became the prototype of the modern business tycoon by establishing the family interests as a public company, expanding its base from banking into mining and the spice trade, and spreading his investments across a wide range of interests, including real estate. He initiated the family's long-running funding of the Habsburgs, providing the bribes which helped Charles I of Spain win election as the Holy Roman Emperor, Charles V in 1519. Although overshadowed by the Fuggers, the Welsers nonetheless ranked among Germany's richest families, and at one time owned all of Venezuela.

During the Reformation, Augsburg was the setting for four events which were to have enormous repercussions throughout Christendom. In 1518, Martin Luther was summoned there to meet the papal legate, Cardinal Tommaso Cajetan, who unsuccessfully attempted to make him retract his 95 theses against Catholic orthodoxy. Twelve years later, with the Reformation already established throughout much of Germany, Charles V called a Diet in an attempt to enforce conformity, with Luther banned for attendance. However, when the Protestant princes refused to acquiesce, the theologian Philipp Melanchthon drew up the Augsburg Confession on their behalf. This document, which remains the basic creed of all Lutheran churches, stated that there was no difference of faith with Catholicism, but seven abuses of practice to which they objected.

When wars failed to reunite the Empire, Charles V tried again in 1547 by means of the Augsburg Interim to enforce conformity. This gave way to the Reformers on the right of priests to marry and for the laity to receive wine and bread at Communion. However, it proved insufficient to placate the Protestants, and Charles was forced to concede defeat by the Peace of Augsburg of 1555, which recognized that Germany was effectively divided into a host of states. From then on, each ruler was free to choose his own religion, and force his subjects to follow suit or move elsewhere, though the Catholic position was safeguarded by forcing ecclesiastic princes to cede their territory if they wished to convert. Only in the Free Imperial Cities were the faiths allowed to coexist, and in Augsburg religious tolerance was demonstrated by the idiosyncratic practice of building new Protestant churches alongside existing Catholic ones.

The city was the only one in Germany which took to heart the Renaissance style, which was introduced as a direct result of the Fuggers' extensive business interests in Italy, and flourished for well over a century. Elias Holl, who served as municipal architect from 1602 to 1635, embellished the city with a magnificent series of public edifices which rank among the greatest and most original Renaissance buildings outside Italy.

The Thirty Years' War saw Augsburg lose well over half its population, but it recovered well in the 18th century, becoming the seat of a prestigious art academy and the site of Europe's first cotton factory. In 1806 the city was incorporated into Bavaria, and was chosen as the administrative seat of the Upper Danube area, which in 1838 was renamed the province of Swabia. It developed as an industrial centre, and was particularly prominent in the field of mechanical engineering, in which the company known by the acronymn MAN (Maschinenfabrik Augsburg-Nürnberg) was dominant. In 1898, Rudolf Diesel invented at its factory the engine which has put his name into languages all over the world.

After World War I, Augsburg's Messerschmidt works became the main hub of German aircraft production. This inevitably meant that the city was a prime target of the Allied bombing missions of 1944-5, which left half of it destroyed, necessitating several decades of painstaking reconstruction work to return its historic monuments to their former splendour.

Augsburg's historic core, one of the largest in Germany, is centred on the spacious cobbled Rathausplatz. The **Rathaus** (Town Hall) itself, a palatial seven-storey structure, is the most magnificent municipal headquarters of any German city. It was built by Elias

Holl between 1615 and 1624 in a highly distinctive idiom which marries Italianate forms with such characteristically German features as octagonal corner towers and onion domes. Atop the central pediment is a carved pine-cone, the city's symbol since Roman times. The main ceremonial chamber, the Goldener Saal (Golden Hall) was almost completely destroyed in 1944, but its resplendent decoration was recreated with the help of old photographs forty years later, in time for the city's 2,000th anniversary celebrations. Its gilded wooden ceiling is adorned with allegorical paintings on the theme of civic and moral virtues. Along the walls are frescoes of Christian and pagan rulers who embodied these traits.

Immediately north of the Rathaus is the **Perlachturm** (Perlach Tower), which dates back to about 1060 and originally served as a watchtower. In 1614-16 it was remodelled by Holl, who raised it to its present height of 70.4m by adding a bell chamber and lantern, above which is a gold-plated weather vane of the goddess Cisa. From the top, there is a wonderful view over the city, one which is particularly helpful for orientation purposes.

The tower dwarfs the adjoining 12th century church of **St Peter am Perlach**, the oldest brick building in Southern Germany, which has been restored to its original Romanesque form following war damage. Inside are life-sized 13th century murals of St Peter, St Paul and two unidentified female saints.

In the middle of Rathausplatz is the marble and bronze **Augustusbrunnen** (Augustus Fountain), which was made between 1588 and 1594 by the Dutch Mannerist sculptor Hubert Gerhard. Above the column is a statue of Augustus Caesar, depicted in the pose adopted for delivering a ceremonial speech. Around the base are allegorical depictions of Augsburg's four rivers. These are the Lech, whose oar symbolizes the city's dependence on navigation; the Wertach, with a cogwheel in honour of the presence of fertile farmland; the Brunnenbach, with a fishing net; and the veiled Singold who bears a cornucopia of fruits.

From the south-west corner of Rathausplatz, Philippine-Welser-Strasse leads to the **Maximilianmuseum**, which occupies a Renaissance patrician mansion with restored sgraffito decoration. It contains superb displays of applied art, ranging from medieval vestments and lapidary fragments via wooden models of Elias

Holl's buildings to the wonderful Baroque and Rococo creations of the goldsmiths, silversmiths and watchmakers who made Augsburg one of Europe's leading producers of luxury goods. Outside the museum is a statue to Hans Jakob Fugger, the only member of the dynasty so honoured. Curiously enough, he was unsuccessful in business, but was a renowned bibliophile, his collections forming the base of what subsequently became the Staatsbibliothek (State Library) in Munich.

A block to the east is the Gothic church of **St Anna**, which was founded in 1321 as part of a Carmelite monastery, and rebuilt in the 1460s following a fire. In 1602 Elias Holl equipped the church, which had been allocated to the Protestants at the Reformation, with a tower built directly over the structure, rather than on a separate base. The same architect later designed the school which stands in the courtyard to the west.

The huge Fuggerkapelle (Fugger Chapel) effectively forms a western chancel. This was endowed in 1507 by Ulrich and Jacob Fugger as a memorial chapel for themselves and their deceased brother Georg. Its unconventional position was the result of skulduggery on both sides of the agreement: the brothers intended it as a self-conscious statement of the family's wealth and power, and aimed to seal off public access, whereas the prior saw it as a means of increasing the church's capacity at no cost to its funds. The sumptuous decorative scheme marked the belated German debut of the full-blown Renaissance style, though it appears to have been the work of local craftsmen.

On the first floor of the cloisters is a museum known as the **Lutherstiege** (Luther Steps) in commemoration of its role as the place where the great Reformer lodged for two weeks at the time of his summons to meet Cardinal Cajetan. The plain chamber designated the Lutherkammer is presumed to be the one where Luther actually stayed. Together with the rooms alongside, and the old monks' gallery, it contains extensive documentation on Augsburg's role in the Reformation.

Maximilianstrasse, Augsburg's showpiece main thoroughfare, runs southwards from the south-east corner of Rathausplatz. Lined with the headquarters of leading municipal and corporation bodies, and with the residences built by the merchants who dominated their affairs, it is named in honour of Emperor Maximilian I, who forged the complex series of dynastic alliances which led to the Habsburg family's dominance in European affairs. Augsburg had a special place in his affections - no doubt because his political scheming was so dependent on the goodwill of the city's bankers.

Towards the top end of the street, a block east of the Maximilianmuseum, is a reproduction of the demolished **Weberzunfthaus** (Weavers' Guildhall), whose exterior is covered with colourful murals illustrating the Battle of Lechfeld and the history of the guild. Facing it across Bürgermeister-Fischer-Strasse is the church of **St Moritz** (St Maurice), which enjoys the patronage of the Fugger family to this day. Badly damaged in the war, it has been stripped of Baroque accretions and returned to its former appearance, an amalgam of Romanesque and Gothic.

Opposite, in an isolated position in the middle of Maximilianstrasse, is the **Merkurbrunnen** (Mercury Fountain), which was made in 1596-9 by Adrian de Vries, another Dutch Mannerist, who was court sculptor to the Habsburgs. The fountain celebrates Augsburg's role as a commercial centre.

A little further down the western side of the street are the **Fuggerhäuser** (Fugger Mansions), a series of three adjoining buildings which together served as the family residence and business headquarters. They were the setting for Luther's meetings with Cajetan, and also served as Charles V's residence during his negotiations with the Protestants in 1548. Following extensive wartime damage, the complex, which remains in the hands of the still-prominent banking dynasty, was rebuilt in a simplified format. The most enchanting feature is the smaller of the two main courtyards, the Damenhof ("Ladies' Court"), which was built in a pure Italian Renaissance style as a venue for games, musical performances and other festive events.

Immediately to the rear of the Fuggerhäuser is the **Zeughaus** (Arsenal), built by Holl in 1602-7 as his first major project as municipal architect. The facade, which may have been designed with the help of the painter Joseph Heintz, is a brilliantly original composition which is uncannily anticipatory of the Baroque style.

South of the Fuggerhäuser is the **Schaezler-Palais**, a sumptuous Rococo palace built between 1765 and 1770 by the Munich architect

Albert von Lespilliez. The original client was a banker, Baron Adam Liebert von Liebenhofen, but it was subsequently acquired by his in-laws, whose name it bears. The Festsaal (Festive Hall), the sumptuous setting for the annual concerts of music by Mozart held in June and July, still preserves its original decoration. Other rooms house a gallery of 16th to 18th century paintings, including Veronese and Tiepolo.

The palace is connected to the former Dominican convent of St Katharina (St Catherine) to the rear, which has been converted to house the **Staatsgalerie** (State Gallery), a collection of German old masters. This is dominated by the work of the 15th and 16th century Augsburg School, whose most prominent members were Hans Holbein the Elder and Hans Burgkmair.

In the middle of Maximilianstrasse, directly opposite the Schaezler-Palais, is the **Herkulesbrunnen** (Hercules Fountain), which Adrain de Vries made in tandem with the Merkurbrunnen. The grandest of all the fountains in the city, it is topped with a sculptural group showing Hercules vanquishing the seven-headed Hydra.

On Dominikanerberg, a block to the west, is the former Dominican monastery church of **St Magdalena** (St Mary Magdalene), built in 1513-15 by Burkard Engleberg, the leading local practitioner of the late Gothic style. Its interior is reminiscent more of a hall than a church, being divided down the central axis by a row of seven columns. Between 1716 and 1724, the Feichtmayr brothers cloaked this with stuccowork, while Johann Georg Bergmüller added the ceiling paintings of the Twelve Mysteries of the Rosary. The church now houses the **Römisches Museum** (Roman Museum), which in fact consists of archaeological finds from the Bronze Age to the Frankish period. Among the highlights are a life-sized bronze head of a horse, which probably formed part of a 2nd century statue of the Emperor Marcus Aurelius, and the 4.5m high pillared tombstone with carvings of four figures which is displayed alongside.

Maximilianstrasse terminates at Ulrichsplatz, which is closed off by the great basilica of **St Ulrich und Afra** (SS Ulrich and Afra). This was founded as a Benedictine monastery in 1006, though the present late Gothic church, which is partly by Burkard Engleberg, was erected between 1477 and 1612. Its Renaissance tower, which reaches a height of 93m, is crowned by the most famous of the onion domes which are such a recurrent feature of the city's skyline. The two saints after which it is named are buried in the crypt: St Afra in a simple sarcophagus, St Ulrich in an ornate Rococo shrine. Augsburg's third patron, St Simpert, who is presumed to have been a nephew of Charlemagne, is buried in a Baroque marble tomb in a chapel on the south side of the nave.

The preaching hall adjoining the north side of the basilica was rebuilt in 1709-10 to serve as the Lutheran church of **St Ulrich** and its cheerful Baroque facade makes an effective foil to its neighbour.

Not far to the south-east, reached via Peter-Kötzer-Gasse, Ulrichsgasse and Am Eser, is another of Augsburg's best-known landmarks, the **Rotes Tor** (Red Gate), whose present appearance is the result of a rebuilding carried out by Elias Holl in 1622. This was the main southern entrance to the city, through which all goods going to and from the Tyrol and Italy had to pass. The bastion beyond now serves as the **Freilichtbühne** (Open-air Theatre).

Immediately to the east is Holl's last major commission, the **Heilig-Geist-Spital** (Holy Ghost Hospital), which was built from 1623-31. It is now home to the internationally celebrated marionette theatre, the Puppenkiste. In the courtyard are three older water towers plus the Brunnenmeisterhaus (Well Master's House). The latter now contains the **Schwäbisches Handwerkermuseum** (Swabian Handicrafts Museum), which has displays on the history of around forty different traditional crafts.

Several of these are still practised in central Augsburg: indeed, no fewer than fifteen different craft workshops, most of which offer demonstrations at least once per week, lie along the Handwerkerweg, a trail devised by the tourist office. The workshops are concentrated in the old artisans' quarter in the eastern part of the city centre. This is crossed by the **Lechkanäle** (Lech Canals), which were dug to provide a ready source of power, as well as for cleansing and refuse disposal.

A reconstruction of one of the old water-wheels can be seen at the top end of the Schwallech, a canal which runs along the side of Schwibbogengasse, a short distance north of the Heilig-Geist-Spital. Just to the north-east is the **Vogeltor** (Bird Gate) of 1445, which guards the preserved eastern section of the Stadtmauer (Town

Wall).

Continuing northwards, the **Färberhaus** (Dyer's House) at Mittlerer Lech 48 is the last of its type in the city; note the loft on the south side with the balcony in which materials were hung out to dry. The **Holbeinhaus** (Holbein House) at Vorderer Lech 20 is a reproduction of the original building on the site, which was destroyed in 1944. Hans Holbein the Younger, the renowned portraitist of the brilliant English court of King Henry VIII, spent his childhood there, his father having established himself as the leading Augsburg painter of the day. Temporary art exhibitions are now held there.

At no. 8 on the same street is the **Komödie** (Comedy Playhouse). This occupies the former home and factory of a cotton manufacturer, which was created in 1764-5 by knocking together several 16th century houses. The **Alte Silberschmiede** (Old Silver Smithy) at Pfladergasse 10 dates back to the mid-16th century and is thus one of the oldest surviving craft workshops in the city. Of special note is the external wooden staircase leading to the upper floors.

A little further north, facing the rear end of the Rathaus across Elias-Holl-Platz, is the Franciscan convent of **Maria Stern**, which was built by Johannes Holl (father of Elias) in late Gothic style in 1574-6. The slender brick belfry is crowned by what is believed to be the earliest example of the Welsche Haube, the distinctive onion dome that is such a recurrent feature of Augsburg's skyline. The interior of the church was remodelled in late Baroque style.

On Perlachberg to the north is the **Stadtmetzg** (Municipal Butchery), built by Elias Holl in 1606-9. It originally served both as the offices of the butchers' guild and as a meat market, with the canal below providing cooling for the meats in storage; it was later the home of the art academy, and is now used by the local administration. The city's coat-of-arms is displayed on the rusticated facade, whose twin portals each have carved ox heads on the door frames.

A short distance to the north-east, at Auf dem Rain 7, is the **Bertolt-Brecht-Haus**, the birthplace of the renowned Communist poet and playwright. His relationship with his native city, which he left for good at the age of 21, was not a happy one. However, he later used it as the backdrop for a short story, *The Augsburg Chalk Circle*, which was subsequently reworked, using the same plot but a different location, into one of his most famous plays, *The Caucasian Chalk Circle*. The small memorial museum presents a photographic record of his career, with an emphasis on his early years.

At the head of Barfüsserstrasse to the south is the Gothic **Barfüsserkirche** (Church of the Barefoot Monks). This was almost totally destroyed in the war, and only the austere, barn-like chancel was rebuilt. It contains an elaborate wrought-iron choir screen and a large Crucifix by the early 17th century sculptor Georg Petel. Tombstones of many prominent local families can be seen in the star-vaulted cloister alongside.

On Jakoberstrasse, the eastern continuation of Barfüsserstrasse, is the main entrance to the **Fuggerei**, the oldest social settlement in the world. It was founded by Jacob Fugger in order to provide housing for "poor, needy citizens of Augsburg", although it now seems that he was at least partly motivated by the opportunity of laundering some of his considerable fortune. Construction work began in 1516 under Thomas Krebs, and the first residents took up occupancy seven years later. It forms a town within a town, closed off from the rest of Augsburg by four gates which are kept locked and guarded by a nightwatchman between 10pm and 5am. The ivy-covered houses are arranged into neat terraces, which have an idyllic, cloistral atmosphere, thanks in no small measure to the absence of traffic. There are now 67 separate dwellings, the number having been increased from 52 as a result of the reconstruction that was necessary to make good the damage suffered in World War II.

Initially, the Fuggerei was intended for families with children, but it has gradually evolved into a community for older people, with 55 being the minimum age to gain admittance. All residents must be Roman Catholic, needy, free of any criminal record, and citizens of Augsburg. Each day they are required to recite the Lord's Prayer, the Ave Maria and the Credo. The rent, which is subsidized by the Fugger family foundations, is permanently frozen at the original rate of one Rhenish guilder or DM1.72 per annum for a three-apartment house; those in the smaller houses reserved for widows pay just DM1. However, modest supplements have to be paid to the local authority for such modern conveniences as running water and street cleaning.

Behind the main gateway is the modest little **Markuskirche** (St

Mark's Church), which was built by Johannes Holl in 1581. Portraits of the family of Markus Fugger, the church's founder, can be seen on the predella of the winged altar. The only other interior open to the public is that of Mittlere Gasse 13, one of the original houses of the settlement. This is now designated the **Fuggereimuseum** and is furnished in a manner that would have been familiar to an inhabitant of the 17th and 18th centuries.

The **Neptunbrunnen** (Neptune Fountain) on Jakobsplatz, opposite the eastern side of the Fuggerei, is the oldest in Augsburg, the bronze figure having been cast in 1536 from a design by Hans Daucher. Back on Jakoberstrasse, facing the Gothic church of **St Jakob** (St James), a former staging-post on the pilgrimage route to Santiago de Compostella, is the **Georgsbrunnen** (St George' Fountain), which dates from 1575. A 15th century gateway, the **Jakobertor** (St James' Gate) closes off the end of the street, guarding the moat which still runs along the eastern perimeter of the historic part of the city.

It is worth following the moat northwards to see the picturesque **Fünfgratturm** (Five Pinnacles Tower) of 1454, which takes its name from the sharply pointed steeples crowning its roof and its four corner turrets, and the **Jakoberbrunnenturm** (St James' Water Tower), which was built by Elias Holl in 1608. Beyond the latter is the **Oblatter Wall**, a defensive system dating from 1540, consisting of an earthworks and a fortified tower. Those wanting to take to the water can hire a rowing boat at the landing stage alongside.

Dominating the northern part of the city centre is the **Dom** (Cathedral), reached from Rathausplatz via Karolinenstrasse and Hoher Weg. The original twin-towered Romanesque structure, which was completed in 1165, adopted the groundplan characteristic of German imperial cathedrals, with choirs at both ends of the building. It was partially Gothicized between 1331 and 1343, a project believed to have been carried out under the direction of Heinrich Parler, the founder of a celebrated dynasty of masons which built many important churches in Germany and Central Europe. In 1356, the same masonic workshop began constructing a brand new east chancel with radiating chapels, though this was not completed until 1431. The southern transept portal, the main entrance to the Dom, is densely packed with the highly expressive sculptures characteristic of the Parler family; the earlier northern portal, though not quite so overwhelming in effect, is also in this style. The famous Romanesque bronze doors have been removed indoors for conservation reasons. From the same period are the five stained glass windows in the nave depicting Old Testament figures.

On the west side of the Dom is the **Fronhof**, the former palace of the Prince-Bishops. Only the tower remains of the late medieval building where the Confession of Augsburg was first presented; the rest of the complex was rebuilt in Baroque style in the first half of the 18th century. Since 1817, the Fronhof has served as the seat of the regional government of the Bavarian province of Swabia. However, the main staircase, with its decorative frescoes by Johann Georg Bergmüller, and the Festsaal (Festive Hall) are accessible to the public, except when required for functions.

On Heilig-Kreuz-Strasse further west are the paired **Heilig-Kreuz-Kirchen** (Holy Cross Churches). The older of these, a late Gothic hall church built between 1492 and 1508, is used for Catholic worship and contains an altarpiece of the Assumption by Rubens. Its Lutheran counterpart, which dates back to the 1650s, features a coffered ceiling, a painted gallery, and several old master paintings, including Tintoretto's "Baptism of Christ".

On Am Katzenstadel, just to the north-west, is the **Giesshaus**, a two-storey hall building erected by Elias Holl in 1601-2. Its tower in the shape of a cannon bore symbolizes its original function as a cannon casting workshop; nowadays it is used by a girls' school. At the end of the same street is the **Wertachbrucker Tor** (Wertach Bridge Gate). The lower parts of this date back to 1370; the two upper storeys, the pyramid roof and the lantern were added by Holl in 1605.

A little to the south-east on Georgenstrasse is the former collegiate church of **St Georg**, which was built in late Gothic style between 1490 and 1505, though the tower and onion dome were not added until 1691. Under the pulpit is a remarkable column with interlaced decoration, a relic of the Romanesque church which previously stood on the site.

At no. 30 on Frauentorstrasse, which runs perpendicular to the eastern side of Georgenstrasse, is the **Mozarthaus** (Mozart House), the patrician mansion where Leopold Mozart, father of Wolfgang

Amadeus, was born in 1717. Even within his own lifetime, he was best known as a Svengali-type figure, but he was also a capable composer in his own right. The house contains documentary material on both father and son, as well as some original furnishings, including a piano by Johann Andreas Stein which is frequently used for recitals.

Further down the same street, Jesuitengasse leads west to the **Kleiner Goldener Saal** (Small Golden Hall), the only surviving part of the former Jesuit seminary, and nowadays a venue for concerts and lectures. It has stuccowork by Johann Michael Feichtmayer and a ceiling fresco by Matthäus Günther illustrating the prophesies of Isiah.

Back on Frauentorstrasse, follow Karmelitengasse and Karmelitenmauer eastwards to reach the so-called **Schwedenstiege** (Swedish Steps), a part of the city wall which gained mythical status in the winter of 1634-5, when Augsburg was besieged by Bavarian troops and suffered a severe famine. A local baker climbed the wall and showed the enemy a newly baked loaf of bread as evidence that the city was not starving. The ruse apparently worked, but the baker was shot and subsequently died from his wounds. A larger-than-life statue, popularly known as the Steinerner Mann (Stone Man), was immediately made in his memory.

A little further north is the tiny 11th century church of **St Gallus**, which is now used by a Russian Orthodox congregation. Outside is a plaque showing the place where Luther fled from the city in fear of his life following his meetings with Cardinal Cajetan in 1518. Further on, at the north-eastern corner of the municipal defences, is the **Bastion Lueginsland**, which was begun in 1430. It commands a fine view over the city and the valley of the Lech.

Of the monuments outside the confines of the historic centre, the **Synagoge** (Synagogue) on Halderstrasse deserves special mention. This imposing Jugendstil (Art Nouveau) complex, grouped around an open courtyard, was built in 1914-17 for what was then one of Germany's largest and most liberal Jewish communities. Nowadays the tiny and very orthodox sect who remain use only the small prayer hall. The domed main temple, which can be viewed from the gallery, and the ancilliary buildings, which house a rich treasury of liturgical items, now serve as a museum of Swabian and Bavarian

Jewish culture.

A little further west is Augsburg's **Hauptbahnhof**, the oldest continuously functioning main train station of any city in the world. Built in 1843-6, it is an imposing example of the architecture of the railway age, with a grandiose facade in the manner of an Italian palazzo.

Rothenburg ob der Tauber, the Reichstadtfest; the Plönlein,
with tableau of Romantic artists

Dinkelsbühl, general view from the east
Creglingen, the Römschlössle

STAGE 11:
AUGSBURG TO DONAUWÖRTH (48km)

The next designated staging-post after Augsburg is Donauwörth, 48km away by the most direct of the various alternative routes, the largest gap of any along the Romantic Road, though there are three places en route which warrant a short stop. For cyclists, this adds up to an ideal length for a day's journey, but for walkers it may be just a bit too much ground to cover without breaking for the night. Unfortunately, accommodation along the way is once again very limited indeed. However, the latter half of the route follows a roughly parallel course to that of the Augsburg to Donauwörth railway. As stopping trains run along this in both directions until late in the evening, there is always a ready-made "escape route".

The track out of Augsburg can be picked up at any point on the right bank of the Lech; from the city centre, the quickest way to join it is via the aforementioned Lechbrücke, just over 1km to the east. As elsewhere along this track, there is little hint of being in a major city, other than the sight of the odd residential apartment block to the right. After 2km or so, the confluence of the Wertach with the Lech can be seen. A little further on, the built-up area peters out completely, and the track passes under the bridge carrying the A8/E52 motorway.

It is then a bit more than 1km to another bridge leading into **GERSTHOFEN**, the northernmost of Augsburg's ring of satellite towns. Here there is a choice of routes, the more scenic of which continues onwards up the same bank of the river. However, it is well worth following the alternative route for the 1km to the town centre: the way lies over the bridge, along Kanalstrasse and Bauernstrasse.

Beyond, at the head of Bahnhofstrasse, is a 30m high water tower, a Jugendstil (Art Nouveau) building of 1906. This is now home to the **Ballon-Museum** (Balloon Museum), the only one of its kind in existence. *Its presence is explained by Gersthofen's role as the international metropolis for ballooning: it is claimed that each year more*

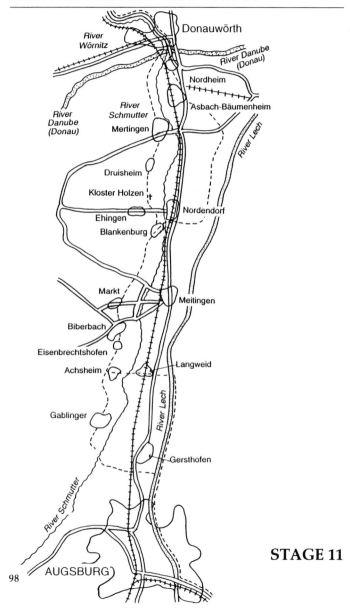

STAGE 11

balloons take off from there than from everywhere else in the world put together. There are five floors of displays: the first is devoted to the history of aeronautics, the second to early balloon flights, while the third is centred on a full-scale model of a balloon. The fourth floor focuses on Gersthofen's place in the history of ballooning, with particular reference to the first-ever excursion into the stratosphere in 1931. An amusing collection of caricatures is also on view, while the floor above focuses on balloons in contemporary art.

One of the marked Romantic Road routes continues through Gersthofen and westwards to Hirblingen, then bears north-west to Batzenhofen and northwards via Gablingen to Achsheim. As the entire 11km of this itinerary lie through featureless farming country, it is far preferable to double back to the bridge, and continue northwards along the right bank of the Lech, which is quite heavily wooded for the first 4km, but then thins out. It is a further 4km to the next bridge, which leads to Langwied, located a short way back from the river.

Having crossed over, the route skirts the southern end of the village, and traverses the railway, which lies to the east for the remainder of the way to Donauwörth. It continues on for 1km to Achsheim, where it crosses the River Schmutter, whose course it thereafter parellels until its confluence with the Danube. In the centre of the village it joins up with the alternative route, and swings round sharply to assume a northerly course. Travelling through the meadows on the eastern side of the wooded Achsheimer Hart, it continues through the hamlet of Eggelhof and the village of Eisenbrechtshofen, from where it descends to **BIBERBACH**, 5km from Achsheim and 22km out of Augsburg.

At the southern edge of this little market town is the **Pfarr- und Wallfahrtskirche Heilig Kreuz** (Parish and Pilgrimage Church of the Holy Cross), built in Baroque style between 1684 and 1697 by Valerian Brenner, an architect from the Voralberg province of Austria. *The tower of the previous Gothic church was retained, but, in order that it should blend with the new building, it was topped with a slender octagon crowned by an onion dome. Entry is via the northern side, which is fronted by a Kalvarienberg (Calvary), with life-sized polychromed figures by Jakob Rill, a sculptor from Augsburg. Work on decorating the interior continued until the 1750s, hence its predominantly Rococo* *appearance. Its focal point, and the goal of the pilgrimages, is the 2.20m high carving of the Crucifixion, a noble Romanesque work from around 1220. The last part of the decoration to be completed was the ceiling, which has stuccowork by Franz Xaver Feichtmayr of Wessobrunn and frescoes by a Tyrolean, Balthasar Riepp, illustrating the legend and dogma of the Holy Cross.*

From the church, the route proceeds downhill to the T-junction in the town centre. It bears right there, and continues to the end of the built-up area, where it makes a sharp turn left, and proceeds northwards along the side of farmland. After 2km it reaches Markt, above which stands a privately owned Schloss with a Baroque church in its grounds. The latter is open for mass on Sunday mornings, but at other times entry is forbidden, and signs warn of the presence of guard dogs.

In the village below, the route swings sharply to the right, then shortly afterwards to the left, and continues northwards along a minor road between woods and fields. After 3km it passes through Kühlenthal; 2km further on it reaches Blankenburg, where it bears right into the centre of the village. Immediately before the bridge over the River Schmutter, there is a choice of routes.

The more circuitous and less scenic of these is intended mainly for campers. It travels eastwards over the bridge to the station at Nordendorf, then over the tracks and east again to Ellgau, which lies just back from the Lech. From there it continues northwards to Oberndorf, then north-westwards via the campsite in Eggelstetten to Asbach and Baumenheim.

The alternative route along the Schmutter valley takes 13km, as opposed to 17km, to cover the same ground. Beyond the northern end of Blankenburg, it follows a farm track through the fields west of the river. This offers a fine view ahead to **HOLZEN**, which is reached by turning left when the track reaches a road, then almost immediately turning right uphill, thus bypassing the village of Ehingen altogether.

Holzen consists of a few houses plus the enormous complex of the former **Benediktinerinnenabtei** (Benedictine Abbey), which has been a mental hospital since 1927. *Founded as far back as 1152, the convent was badly damaged in the Thirty Years' War, and was completely rebuilt in Baroque style. The twin-towered church, entered from the rear* *courtyard, was built between 1696 and 1704.*

Leaving Holzen, the route continues 1km uphill to skirt the western edge of Allmannshofen, a village which stretches over to the opposite side of the Schmutter. There is then a gentle 2km descent, passing briefly through the Mertinger Forst, to Druisheim. At the end of this village, the signposted route takes a sharp detour east from the road, and goes along a farm track downhill to the little town of Metingen, another 2.5km on. Beyond the riding centre, it turns left, then makes a right turn at the dairy, so bypassing the centre. Once out of town, it follows a farm track, which continues to a road, where it turns right then left on to another track, with a fine view of Donauwörth directly ahead. Skirting the western fringe of Bäumenheim, it meets up with the alternative route from Blankenburg at the north-western edge of the village.

The track continues through meadows along the western bank of the Schmutter. After 2km, it bears right, crosses the road at the entrance to Nordheim, then travels along the side of the railway tracks for a few hundred metres, before crossing under the tunnel. It then enters the southernmost outskirts of Donauwörth and crosses the Danube (Donau), the one and only encounter the Romantic Road has with this great river. Just to the left, the Wörnitz - a recurrent feature of the next stage of the route - flows into the Danube to the west. Once over the bridge, a sharp left turn into Kapellstrasse leads to the town centre.

Donauwörth

DONAUWÖRTH came into existence in the Dark Ages as a fishing settlement on the little island of Werth, which is actually located in the Wörnitz, rather than in the Danube, as its name would imply. Its modern history, however, is deemed to begin in 977, the estimated date of the construction of the first bridge over the Danube. By the 11th century, it had expanded on to the northern bank of the Wörnitz, though the town continued to be known as Werth, or Schwäbischwerth ("Swabian Werth"). A municipal charter was granted in 1193, and in 1301 it gained the status of a Free Imperial City. This privilege was suddenly withdrawn in 1607 when a dispute between the local Protestant majority and the Catholic minority erupted into violence. The town was annexed by Bavaria,

Catholicism was restored as the main religion, and it was given its present name. While this sealed Donauwörth's fate as a provincial Bavarian town, which it has remained ever since, the event had much wider repercussions, serving as the catalyst for the Thirty Years' War, which defined the future course of German history.

A tour of the town, whose current population is around 18,000, can conveniently begin on Kapellstrasse, immediately over the Danube bridge. In the park by the waterside is the **Junge Donau**, an allegorical figure of the still-young river in the guise of a nude woman. It was created in 1985 by Hans Wimmer, a Munich sculptor steeped in the tradition of Classical antiquity. Further down the same street is the **Deutschordenshaus** (House of the Teutonic Knights), a Neoclassical building of 1774-8 which served as the local headquarters of the eponymous order, which first established a base in the town in 1214.

From the end of Kapellstrasse, Spitalgasse leads down to the **Rieder Tor** (Ried Gate), the only survivor of the four main gateways which guarded the town wall. It takes its name from the island across the narrow channel known as the Kleine (ie. Little) Wörnitz, whose name has been changed from Werth to Ried. In its present form, the gateway dates back to 1811, and is an impressive example of Neoclassical architecture. The upper storeys house the local history collections of the **Haus der Stadtgeschichte** (House of Town History), but in common with all but one of Donauwörth's museums, this is only open at weekends.

From the Rieder Tor, an alley named Benzberg leads west to the **Fäbertörl** (Dyers' Little Gate), whose archway gives access to a pleasant promenade along the Kleine Wörnitz. To the left is a humpback wooden bridge giving access to the quiet backstreets of Ried. The prominent russet-coloured building in the foreground is known as the Hintermeierhaus after its last private owners, and was formerly the residence of prosperous fishing, shipping or farming families. It now contains the **Heimatmuseum** (Local Museum), which has extensive collections of locally produced ceramics and ironware, as well as a wide range of exhibits illustrating the culture and lifestyle of Donauwörth residents in times past. The annexe has a permanent exhibition on the town of Lovrin in the Banat region of Romania, an area settled by large numbers of Germans in the 18th

Donauwörth, the Rieder Tor

century.

Returning to the Rieder Tor along Hindenburgstrasse, Spitalgasse leads back up to the **Rathaus** (Town Hall), which has occupied the same site since 1236. The building has been altered on many subsequent occasions, and owes its present appearance to a Neo-Gothic remodelling carried out in 1853. Its glockenspiel can be heard daily at 11am and 4pm, when it plays a medley of tunes, including an aria from the opera *The Magic Violin* by the 20th century composer Werner Egk, a native of Donauwörth.

Directly ahead lies the upwardly sloping **Reichsstrasse** (literally, "Imperial Street"), the town's majestic main thoroughfare. Along with much of the centre, it was reduced to rubble in two bombing raids in the closing weeks of World War II, but was later immaculately restored to its former appearance. At the foot of the western side of the street is the half-timbered **Baudrexlhaus**, whose weather-vane bears the date 1592. Directly opposite is the **Stadtzoll** (Town Customs House), a gabled Gothic mansion of 1418 which also housed the office of the burgomaster and the drinking chamber of the town councillors. Under the bay window is a carving, dated 1524, of a knight carrying a flag and a shield with the municipal coat-of-arms. This is presumed to be a portrait of Georg von Zusum, a local councillor who served as a captain in the Swabian War of 1499.

Further up the same side of the street, at no. 16, is **Café Engel**, which occupies a building which is known to have existed in 1297, making it the oldest surviving house in town. Further on, at no. 32, is the **Stadtkommandantenhaus** (Town Commandant's House), which acquired its present Baroque appearance in the 18th century. Alongside is the gabled **Tanzhaus** (Dance House), which was built around 1400. Its ground floor originally housed shops and a market hall, while upstairs was the municipal festive hall. Nowadays it contains offices, a theatre, a prestigious restaurant and the **Archäologisches Museum** (Archaeological Museum), which has exhibits ranging from the Stone Age to the early medieval period.

Across the street is the **Liebfrauenmünster** (Minster of Our Lady), which was built in the Gothic hall church style between 1444 and 1467. It was the attempted appropriation of this church by the local Protestants in 1608 which set in train the events which eventually led to the Thirty Years' War. The tower, the dominant landmark of Donauwörth's skyline, can be ascended on Sundays between May and September. Its bell chamber houses the "Pummerin", which was cast in 1512 and weighs 131cwt, making it the largest in the province of Swabia. Among the church's furnishings are 15th century stained glass windows; a tabernacle and a font, both dated 1503; and a number of epitaphs to members of the order of Teutonic Knights. Outside the church is the **Reichstadtbrunnen** (Imperial City Fountain), made by Hans Wimmer in 1977 as part of the celebrations commemorating Donauwörth's first millennium.

Framing the top end of Reichsstrasse from the corner of Pflegstrasse and Heilig-Kreuz-Strasse is the spectacularly gabled **Fuggerhaus** (Fugger House), built in 1539 for the famous Augsburg banking dynasty, and nowadays the seat of the local government administration. To the rear are the **Invalidenkaserne** (Invalid Barracks), which were originally built in 1715-16 for quartering a garrison of 400 men, and were taken over as an infirmary for the sick in 1803. The row of wooden balconies at the back is one of Donauwörth's quietest and most picturesque corners.

At the far end of Heilig-Kreuz-Strasse is the former **Heilig-**

Kreuz-Kloster (Holy Cross Monastery). This began life as a nunnery founded in 1028 by Count Mangold I of Werd for the veneration of a fragment of the Holy Cross gifted by Emperor Constantine VIII of Byzantium. Its original location was beside the now vanished feudal castle, Burg Mangold, in the north of town. In 1067 it moved to the present spot, and in 1101 it was converted into a Benedictine monastery. The lower part of the 12th century church tower still survives, but otherwise the complex was rebuilt in Baroque style: the monastic quarters in 1696-8, the church in 1717-20 by the Wessobrunn architect Joseph Schmuzer.

Returning to the Fuggerhaus, Pflegstrasse curves northwards to the former Capuchin monastery, which now houses the **Käthe-Kruse-Museum**. Käthe Kruse gained sudden fame as a result of the sensational reception accorded the soft textile dolls (originally created for her own children) she displayed at the 1912 Berlin exhibition of self-made toys. She set up a factory in Bad Kösen, but when this fell into the Soviet sector after World War II, her son established a new venture in Donauwörth. It is still going strong, and remains loyal to its tradition of all products being entirely hand-made. On view are some 130 toys and shop window mannequins produced by the present and original factories. There are also reconstructions of the workshops, old and new, as well as archive video material.

DONAUWÖRTH TO HARBURG (15km)

The Romantic Road leaves Donauwörth from the north-western end of town. From the centre, the easiest exit is to go all the way down Pflegstrasse, continue a short distance down its northern extension, Berger Vorstadt, and then turn left into Salingerstrasse. At the end of this, ignore the left fork which branches round to the bridge over the Wörnitz, and instead bear right: the track to follow lies straight ahead, parallel to the northern bank of the river.

This side, although well away from any roads, is a mellow landscape of market gardens, fields, and scanty woods; the opposite bank, on the other hand, is often marshy and generally bleaker. After 2km, the path reaches Weinberg, an isolated outlying suburb of Donauwörth, then continues on for 1km to the hamlet of Felsheim, from where it loops round to Wörnitzstein, a village 6km from Donauwörth straddling both sides of the river. Crossing over the bridge, the route continues northwards between the Wörnitz and the railway embankment for 2km to Ebermergen.

In the centre of the village, it crosses over the bridge to the right bank of the Wörnitz and traverses the B25 road. For the 2km to the hamlet of Brünsee it closely hugs the bank through the river's extravagant loop. Beyond, it cuts through the fields before rejoining the river by a pocket of woodland to enter **HARBURG**, 15km from Donauwörth and the Romantic Road's next official staging-post. There are two ways of reaching the town centre. The first is to cross over the first bridge, the Neue Brücke (New Bridge), then continue along Donauwörther Strasse, which is lined with some impressive old houses, notably no. 12, which dates back to the 15th century and was for long the residence of the local Protestant pastor. However, an even more atmospheric approach is to continue on to the car-free Alte Brücke (Old Bridge) or Steinerne Brücke (Stone Bridge), a graceful arched construction of 1712. It commands wonderful views over the town, and is lined with some fine houses, one of which was formerly a mill.

Harburg

Rothenburg apart, this is arguably the most picturesquely sited town on the Romantic Road, spanning as it does both sides of the Wörnitz as well as the wooded slopes of the Burgberg, which rises almost directly above the west bank. The two rail bridges, the road bridge, the footbridge, the hillside tunnels and the flyovers all help to endow it with a grandeur out of all proportion to its size: just 6,000 people live in the municipality, and fewer than 2,500 in the town proper. It rewards a leisurely exploration, and is certainly worth scheduling as an overnight stop, the proximity of both Donauwörth and Nördlingen notwithstanding, as it has some delightful places to stay.

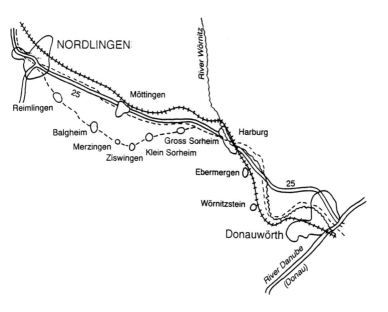

STAGES 12 & 13

Several picturesque buildings, some of them half-timbered, can be seen on the central Marktplatz and the little streets surrounding it. The mansion at no. 8 on Egelseestrasse, which leads off the northeast corner of the square, was built in 1754 as a synagogue for the growing Jewish community, which by the following century amounted to a third of the total population. Closely hugging the hillside off the western end of Marktplatz is the church of St Barbara. This was built in 1612, and is thus an early example of a parish church specially designed for the requirements of Protestant worship.

Schloss Strasse leads steeply uphill to a car park, from where a footpath continues up to the **Schloss**, which dominates the landscape for miles around. It was first documented in 1150 as a possession of the Hohenstaufen Emperors. In 1251 it was granted to the Counts of Oettingen, and remains in the control of the same dynasty to this day.

Entry to the inner courtyard is via the Oberes Tor (Upper Gate), which still preserves its portcullis. Alongside is the Burgvogtei, a former administration building which is now a very reasonably priced hotel and restaurant. In the middle of the precinct is a well, which was formerly 130m deep, though only the first 50m of this survive.

To see the interiors, it is necessary to go to the Pfisterei (Bakery) to buy a ticket for a guided tour. Provided there is sufficient demand, these are offered in English as well as German. They begin with the church of St Michael, which preserves much of its Romanesque interior. There are tombs of members of the House of Oettingen, and fine Gothic carvings of the Madonna and Child and St Michael.

The tour continues in an anticlockwise direction along the Wehrgang (sentry walk), which is equipped with three different types of opening from which counter-attacks could be launched. Both the Weisser Turm (White Tower), which houses a collection of historic weapons, and the Gefängnisturm (Prison Tower) are visited en route to the Kastenhaus (literally, "Box House"), which houses the courtrooms as well as stables and a granary. Next in line is the Bergfried (Keep), otherwise known as the Diebsturm (Thieves' Tower) because of its dungeons and torture chamber. In total contrast is the Saalbau (Hall Building) alongside, which is built on

Harburg, the Alte Brücke and the Schloss

to a second keep, the Faulturm. The Grosser Saal (Great Hall) was built for Albrecht Ernst II, the last of the Oettingen-Oettingen line, whose service as an Imperial Field Marshal is commemorated by the stuccowork allegories of war and peace.

A separate ticket is necessary in order to visit the **Kunstsammlung** (Art Collection), which is housed in the Fürstenbau (Princes' Building), the splendid Renaissance palace at the eastern end of the courtyard. Although some of the most valuable items were recently sold in order to fund maintenance work, there is still a distinguished array of paintings, sculpture and decorative art, predominantly from the German Middle Ages.

HARBURG TO NÖRDLINGEN (20km)
(See map p106/7)

The Romantic Road leaves Harburg via Nördlinger Strasse, which leads northwards from Marktplatz. A track runs along the left-hand side of the B25, and for the first 3km this closely follows the course of the Wörnitz, but starts to branch away at the village of Hoppingen, which is bypassed by the road.

At this point, the geologically distinctive area known as the **Ries** is entered. *It was formed 15,000,000 years ago, when a meteorite crashed down on the mountain plateau previously located there, falling at a speed of around 100,000km/h, and with an impact 250,000 times that of the Hiroshima bomb. It produced a transient crater which, as a result of the evaporation of the meteorite itself and the rocks it hit, gradually spread to cover an almost circular area 25km in diameter. In the process, a new type of rock, known as suevite, came into existence. A shallow lake formed in the crater, but this silted up over the course of the next 2,000,000 years.*

Following the last glaciation period, the present landscape gradually emerged, flat and virtually treeless, with some highly distinctive rocky outcrops amid extremely fertile soils. The Ries is among the world's largest craters, and has been studied more than any other. As it shares many characteristics with the craters of the moon, the astronauts of NASA's Apollo 14 and 17 missions came there in 1971 to undertake preparatory research.

Outside Hoppingen, the Romantic Road waymarks point in two different directions, signifying a choice of routes. Unfortunately, neither of these offers an auspicious introduction to the strange but undoubted charms of the Ries, passing as they do through relentlessly flat farmland. The main attraction of the direct route is its relative brevity: for the remaining 13km to Nördlingen it continues to follow the B25 and the parallel railway, travelling along a special track alongside it for almost the whole way, save for one short diversion into the fields. Some 4km beyond Hoppingen, it enters Möttingen, and passes right through the middle of the village, the only settlement along this part of the road. A further 4km on, it switches from the left to the right side of the road, and 2km later reaches the southern suburbs of Nördlingen, from where it continues onwards to enter the historic part of the town at the Reimlinger Tor.

The alternative route adds an extra 3km to the length of the journey, and is no more scenic. It follows a minor road which performs a loop round six agricultural villages, which are spaced out at distances of between 1km and 3km. Successively, these are Gross Sorheim, Klein Sorheim, Ziswingen, Merzingen, Balgheim and Reimlingen. From the last named, which is much the biggest of these villages, there is a cycle track alongside the road for the first part of the remaining 4km to Nördlingen. The B25 is joined in the outskirts of town, just south of the Reimlinger Tor.

Nördlingen
NÖRDLINGEN, the main town of the Ries, is located at the very heart of the crater. The Romans established a fortified camp on the spot in the 1st century AD, but this was abandoned in 233. The site was resettled by the Alemannian tribe, probably in the 6th century, and the name Nordilinga is first mentioned in 898, as a royal court of the Carolingian dynasty. In 1215, Nördlingen gained the status of a Free Imperial City. Four years later, it initiated its rapid development into one of Germany's leading trading centres by establishing a fair which featured textiles, furs and metal goods in addition to agricultural products.

As a result of the town's continuing expansion, Emperor Ludwig the Bavarian issued an order in 1327 for the construction of a municipal wall to enclose the suburbs that had grown up outside the original fortifications. These were built in the distinctive shape of an almost perfect circle, as the unique nature of the Ries meant that the topographical obstacles most other towns had to overcome when building their defences simply did not exist.

Nördlingen first adopted the Reformation as early as 1522, and continued to prosper right up until the Thirty Years' War. This protracted series of conflicts had a devastating effect on many of Germany's city-states, but none suffered more than Nördlingen. In 1634 there was a landmark battle just outside the town which saw the Protestants, who had hitherto held the upper hand, soundly defeated by the combined forces of the Imperial army and Spain. By the end of the war in 1648, Nördlingen's population was reduced to less than half of its previous figure of around 9,000, and the town sank into decay. It lost its civic independence in 1803, when it was incorporated into Bavaria, but this brought no upturn in its fortunes. Not until 1939 did its population reach the level it had been in its heyday.

Since the end of World War II, which it came through almost undamaged, matters have greatly improved. The town has profited from the general prosperity of postwar Germany, and its population has more than doubled, though this is in large part due to the absorption of outlying villages. While its wonderful heritage of medieval buildings attracts plenty of visitors, it is not swamped by tourists to the same extent as the Romantic Road's other showpiece walled towns, Dinkelsbühl and Rothenburg.

The **Stadtmauer** (Town Wall) is in essence that built in the 14th century by order of Emperor Ludwig, though it was altered and strengthened on several subsequent occasions. It is easily the most complete in Germany; not only does it preserve all five gateways, plus eleven towers and a bastion, it is the only one in the country to retain the entire length of the **Wehrgang** (sentry walk).

There are three ways of walking round the 3km radius of the Stadtmauer. All are worth doing, as the perspectives they offer are so different. The streets immediately within the perimeter of the walls not only enable the sentry walk to be seen to best effect; they are also very picturesque in themselves. On many stretches there are rows of cottages, known as Kasarmen, built directly on to the walls. These were inhabited by soldiers at times when there was the threat of a siege. The sentry walk itself, which is a covered walkway for all but a short stretch, commands a wonderful series of views over the town and its main landmarks, and offers glimpses of the Ries through the battlements.

To see the actual fortifications to best effect, it is necessary to walk along the outside perimeter. Because the land immediately outside is put to a wide variety of uses - as a public promenade, a car park, a children's play area, and as private gardens and orchards - the path at times passes directly alongside the wall, and at times at some distance away, at one point going along the earthen embankment which served as an additional line of defence.

The obvious place to start is the **Reimlinger Tor** (Reimlingen Gate), where the Romantic Road enters from Donauwörth. This belongs to the original 14th century defences, and is thus the oldest of the gates, though both the superstructure and the outer bailey, which bears the municipal coat-of-arms, were later additions. Proceeding in an anticlockwise direction, the **Reissturm** is next in line. This round tower was built at the beginning of the 15th century, and equipped with firing positions towards the end of the Thirty Years' War. At around the same time, the superstructure and cupola were added to the next gateway, the **Deininger Tor** (Deiningen Gate). This was the most vulnerable of the five, being the only one without a firing platform.

The distinctive shape of the Deininger Tor, a cylindrical tower resting on a square base, was followed in the far bulkier **Löpsinger Tor** (Löpsingen Gate) guarding the road from Nuremberg, which assumed its present form at the end of the 16th century. It has an honoured place in local folklore; the legend goes that the feudal lord of the surrounding countryside, Count Hans of Oettingen, decided to take control of the free city. He bribed the nightwatchmen to leave the Löpsinger Tor unbolted, thus allowing his troops to pass within the walls. However, a weaver's wife spotted a stray sow pushing against the entrance gateway, thereby opening it; the alarm was raised, the town saved from invasion and the traitors executed. Nowadays, the gateway houses the Stadtmauermuseum (Town Wall Museum), which is open on summer weekends. In addition to the exhibition of plans, woodcuts, engravings and photographs illustrating the history of the wall, there are fine views to be enjoyed from the balcony.

The next landmark is the plain **Unterer Wasserturm** (Lower Water Tower), which guards the Neue Mühle (New Mill) and the Eger-Kanal (Eger Canal). A short distance further on is the **Spitzturm** (Pointed Tower), which takes its name from its spiky conical roof. This actually stands in front of the Stadtmauer, being connected to it by a rooted passage, and for a time served as a private dwelling. Further on are two of the so-called **Backofentürme** (Baking-oven Towers), horseshoe-shaped projections added in the 16th century.

The **Baldinger Tor** (Baldingen Gate), which guards the

Dinkelsbühl road, was badly damaged in the Thirty Years' War. After the tower finally collapsed in 1703, it was rebuilt as a simple Baroque gateway. Four further Backofentürme line the next section of wall, followed by the **Oberes Wasserturm** (Upper Water Tower), which commands the western side of the Eger-Kanal. A short way to the south, providing extra cover on what was deemed to be a vulnerable stretch, is the ivy-covered **Löwenturm** (Lion Tower), otherwise known as the **Pulverturm** (Powder Tower).

The austere **Berger Tor** (Hill Gate), the western entrance to the town, has both inner and outer gateways. It was built in 1436, and strengthened in 1574-5, when the firing balustrades were added. There is then a fairly long stretch of uninterrupted wall until the **Feilturm**, a 14th century tower with a square base and two round upper storeys. Completing the circuit is the 16th century **Alte Bastei** (Old Bastion), which now serves as an open-air theatre.

Within the Stadtmauer, the overwhelmingly dominant monument is the late Gothic **Georgskirche** (St George's Church), and in particular its 90m high tower, popularly known as the Danielturm, which is visible throughout the Ries. The largest suevite building in the world, the church occupies the bull's-eye position in the town's circular plan, and all the main streets radiate towards it. Its main body, a classic example of the German hall church design, was constructed between 1427 and 1505, and shows a remarkable sense of unity, despite the involvement of many different master masons throughout the construction period.

Work on the Daniel went on until 1539, 17 years after the church had been taken over by the Protestants. The upper part of the tower, a three-storey octagon crowned by a cupola with an open lantern, shows an awareness of the new Renaissance style. Two full-time watchmen still live in the quarters below the observation platform, and every half-hour between 10pm and midnight the traditional call, "So, G'sell, So" ("All's well, fellows, all's well") is sounded. From the balcony, there is a magnificent view embracing not only Nördlingen but also the entire extent of the Ries, which at this height can be seen very clearly to be a crater surrounded by Jurassic plateaux. A total of 99 Ries villages can be seen, as well as such natural features as the rocky outcrop above Wallerstein to the north, and a curious wedge-shaped hill, the Ipf, to the west.

Nördlingen, view from the Danielturm, with the Rathaus in the foreground

Immediately north of the church is the main square, Marktplatz. On its western side is the **Tanzhaus** (Dance House), built in 1442-4 to serve as both the festive hall and the trade fair headquarters. Its upper storey and attic are good examples of half-timbering. Between two of the windows on the first floor is a statue of the Emperor Maximilian I, who had a special affinity with the town. Opposite is the Hotel Zur Sonne ("To the Sun"). It was built in the mid-14th century, and was the place where emperors normally lodged when visiting Nördlingen.

To the north is the **Rathaus** (Town Hall), which has served as such since 1382, though it was originally a trading hall. The tower was added in 1509, the Renaissance stairway to the rear in 1618. On the latter is the so-called Narrenspiegel (Fool's Mirror). Below a relief of a jester is the legend, "Nun sind unser zwey" ("Now there are two of us" - ie. him and whoever is looking at him). Some departments of the local administration, including the tourist office, are housed in the 16th century **Leihhaus** ("Lending House") to the rear of the Rathaus, whose name comes from the role it briefly played in the 19th century.

The next square north of Marktplatz is the Tändelmarkt ("Bric-a-brac Market"). On its northern side is the **Klösterle** ("Little Monastery"), which from 1233 until the secularization of 1536 was occupied by a community of Barefooted Franciscan friars. In the 1580s, the building was converted to serve as the municipal corn store. In 1975, the building was converted again, this time to serve as a festival hall.

Further north lies the Gerberviertel (Tanners' Quarter). Its finest houses, such as the **Lippacher Haus** at Vordere Gerbergasse 25, are characterized by windowless upper storeys or galleries, where the products were hung out to dry. At the western end of the same street is the **Spitalhof** (Hospital Court), an extensive complex of buildings incorporating a small 14th century church with frescoes of the same period.

The rear buildings now house the **Stadtmuseum** (Town Museum). This has an excellent collection of Gothic and Renaissance paintings on the ground floor, dominated by the local masters Friedrich Herlin and Hans Schäufelin. Among the works by the former is a set of panels of the Legend of St George, which was originally the back of the high altar in the church of the same name.

On Hintere Gerbergasse to the rear is a medieval barn, which has been converted to house the state-of-the-art **Rieskrater-Museum** (Ries Crater Museum). This utilizes stone samples as well as charts, models, photographs and video shows to illustrate all facets of the formation, historical development, geology and excavation of the crater.

Returning to Marktplatz, it is a short walk west to Weinmarkt, which is lined with patrician mansions of the Renaissance period. In the middle stands the **Hallgebäude**, a huge gabled building with four corner oriels. It was built in the 1540s as a store for salt and wine; nowadays it houses the municipal archives. Down Neubaugasse, at the corner with Bräugasse, is one of the town's finest half-timbered buildings, the 17th century **Wintersches Haus**. Its courtyard side has three storeys of flower-strewn open galleries. A block to the south is the **Salvatorkirche** (Saviour's Church), which was built in 1422 as part of a Carmelite monastery, and has since 1825 served as the parish church of the local Catholic minority. It has a richly carved entrance portal, with a tympanum of the Last Judgment.

Outside the Stadtmauer, the only point of interest is the **Bayeriches Eisenbahnmuseum** (Bavarian Railway Museum) in the station yards, which is open on Sundays only. It has a fine collection of historic locomotives and rolling stock. Some of these are used for the special steam excursions run on selected summer weekends. These travel along two intact lines no longer used for passenger scheduled services: north-east to Ansbach via Oettingen, and north along the Romantic Road route to Wallerstein, Dinkelsbühl and Feuchtwangen, then on to Crailsheim.

STAGE 14:
NÖRDLINGEN TO WALLERSTEIN (4km)

It is little more than 4km from Nördlingen to Wallerstein, the next designated staging-post on the Romantic Road, but thereafter it is a further 36km (much of it through some of the remotest countryside on the entire Romantic Road route), to Dinkelsbühl. As Wallerstein warrants a visit of several hours, walkers would be well advised to see it one day (whether by stopping for the night, or by making a special trip out from Nördlingen), leaving the whole of the next day free for the next stage.

Exiting Nördlingen via the Baldinger Tor, the route lies over the railway tracks and all the way through Baldingen, formerly a separate village, but now a Nördlingen suburb. At its northern end, the cycle track deviates to the right away from the B25, but soon bears leftwards to rejoin the road just south of Ehringen, another village which has been swallowed up by Nördlingen. From there, a cycle track runs alongside the road for the remaining 1km to **WALLERSTEIN**.

Wallerstein
This town was originally known as Steinheim, and was first documented as such in 1238. It was granted to the territorially ambitious Counts of Oettingen in 1261, and after the Reformation became the main seat of the Catholic branch of the dynasty, the House of Oettingen-Wallerstein. The family gained international renown in the 18th century through musical patronage: both Haydn and Mozart were guests, and the court orchestra, which was directed by the Bohemian composer Franz Anton Rosetti, was considered among the finest in Europe. In 1774, Oettingen-Wallerstein was raised to the rank of a principality, but it failed to survive Napoleon's reordering of the map of Germany, being incorporated into Bavaria in 1806.

Nonetheless, the family retains considerable wealth and influence to this day, numbering landed estates, a brewery and a furniture-

STAGES 14 & 15

making business among its diverse interests. Indeed, so visible is its dominance of the local economy that Wallerstein, whose entire municipal area has a population of little more than 3,000, still manages to maintain the air of a tiny princely capital.

The B25 runs along Wallerstein's main street, Hauptstrasse. In the middle of this stands the **Dreifaltigkeitssäule** (Holy Trinity Column), commissioned in thanksgiving for the town's deliverance from the plague, and carved in 1722-5 by Johann Georg Bschorr.

Herrnstrasse leads up from Hauptstrasse to the **Schloss**, a modest U-shaped residential palace. It acquired its present appearance in 1805, following a remodelling which incorporated various older buildings, including the St-Anna-Kapelle (St Anne's Chapel). The grander of the two main wings, with the clock tower and sundial, is still inhabited by the family; the other contains an extensive collection of 18th and 19th century European and Oriental porcelain and glass, which can be visited by guided tour.

In the Schlosspark, the English-style garden to the west, are three more courtly buildings, though neither the Moritzschlösschen, a small palace which is the home of the dowager princess, nor the Teehaus (Tea House) is accessible to the public. However, the **Reitschule** (Riding School) at the southern end of the park is open for guided visits. It was modelled on the famous Spanish Riding School in Vienna, and built from 1741-51 by a Viennese architect, Paul Ulrich Trientel. The central bloc is an oval-shaped riding hall which is still in regular use for the training of horses and ponies. In the western wing is a collection of historic carriages and sleighs, the star pieces being the three Oettingen-Wallerstein state coaches, notably that made in 1789 for use on festive occasions. There are also harnesses, reins and saddles, plus an old fire engine and other firefighting equipment.

From the western side of Herrnstrasse, steps lead up to Am Kapellberg, on which stands the **Maria-Hilf-Kapelle**, which was built in 1625 on the model of the original rotunda in Klosterlechfeld. At the top of the same street is the **Beamtenhaus** (Administration Building), which still serves its original function as the headquarters of the businesses owned by the Oettingen-Wallerstein family. To the west is Sperlingstrasse, the town's prettiest street, lined by houses built at the end of the 18th century for the estate workers.

Each is topped with the ubiquitous Wallerstein trademark, a mansard roof.

At the top of the town is the site of the medieval castle. The lower ring of outbuildings survives, and houses the brewery, the Fürstenbräu, and the associated restaurant, the Fürstliches Keller. Although the fortress itself was dismantled by the Swedes in the Thirty Years' War, it is well worth climbing to the top of the **Wallersteiner Felsen** (Wallerstein Rocks), one of the distinctive rocky outcrops of the Ries. They stand 65m above the town and command a panoramic view over the region.

WALLERSTEIN TO DINKELSBÜHL (36km)
(See map p120)

To pick up the route out of Wallerstein, it is necessary to return to the eastern edge of town, which can be reached by following Weinstrasse downhill from the Beamtenhaus. Once over the seldom-used rail line, there is a track leading west through a field for about 1km, after which it makes a sharp turn right to assume a northerly course for the remaining 1km to Birkhausen.

It then follows a minor road for another 3km to **MAIHINGEN**. The main part of the village lies to the right, while immediately to the left is the former **Minoritenkloster** (Minorite Monastery). *This order of Franciscan monks first settled the site in 1607, taking over a defunct nunnery. In 1703, work began on replacing the old Gothic buildings with a new Baroque complex designed by Ulrich Beer. The church belongs to the last construction phase of 1712-19, though work on its interior decoration continued for many decades. While monastic life ended with the Napoleonic suppression, and has never been revived, the monastery has been put to a variety of uses. Since 1984, it has gained an appropriate new role as an evangelical Catholic conference centre.*

*The building north of the church, which was once the monks' brewery, now houses the **Rieser Bauernmuseum** (Ries Farming Museum), which has exhibits on all aspects of rural life in the district. Further exhibits can be seen in the annexe, the former workshop and storage buildings to the east of the church.*

The Romantic Road leave Maihingen by the former monastery gate, from where the path loops round to travel westwards along the northern side of a small stream. After about 1km, it reaches a mill, from where it crosses over the railway to join up with a minor road, which is followed for 2km to **MINDEROFFINGEN**. In the middle of the village is the Romanesque **Pfarrkirche St Laurentius** (Parish Church of St Lawrence), the oldest church in the Ries, probably dating from the early 12th century. *It was designed for defence as well as worship, as is evident from the severe plain walls of the* *facade and apse, and the high placement of the main windows in the nave. The populace could take refuge in the stone gallery inside, to which access is controlled by the so-called "one man gate" in the nave's north side.*

At the western edge of Minderoffingen, the route crosses over the B25 and continues for about 200m down the minor road on the other side, before branching off to the right. This leads alongside the Oberholz, one of the patches of woodland marking the end of the Ries. After 2km, the village of Enslingen is reached. From this point, the route assumes a mazy course which is maintained throughout the next 15km, which lies through quiet, totally unspoiled countryside.

After travelling for 2km through a narrow depression between two woods, it arrives at the tiny village of **RAUSTETTEN**. This has a little-known Baroque gem in the former pilgrimage church of **St Blasius**, which now serves the local parish. *Built in 1685-8 by Christian Thumb, it contains a full complement of period furnishings, including high altar, side altars, pulpit, organ and painted tribune gallery. The stuccowork includes angels' heads, acanthus leaves, flowers, scrollwork, vases, a dove representing the Holy Ghost and a scene of the Immaculate Conception.*

Just beyond the western edge of Raustetten, the route proceeds along a forest track to the right, which leads in 1.5km to the Grünhof farm, where there is a junction. It continues ahead, bearing north-east towards the B25. A short distance before reaching the main road, it comes to another junction, and branches off sharply to the left. Here it leaves Swabia and enters another Bavarian province, Middle Franconia (Mittelfranken). It travels west for about 1km to a T-junction, then left again to pass all the way through Rühlingstetten. At the western end of the village, the route turns sharp right to assume a northerly course once more.

It descends down the side of a wood, turns left then right along twisting farm tracks which gradually bear north-west to travel alongside the rail line to the edge of Greiselbach. Instead of crossing the railway to enter the village, which is bisected by the B25 road, the route turns sharp left and goes south-westwards through fields to a coniferous wood, where it swings round to a north-westerly direction again.

In the centre of Wittenbach, it turns right and continues north-westwards through more fields and woodlands to Mönchsroth. At the southern edge of this village, there is a worthwhile signposted detour to see a reconstructed fragment of the Limes, the great fortification system erected by the Romans to delineate and protect the Germanic territories under their control.

The zigzag course of the previous stretch is abandoned for the remaining 8km to Dinkelsbühl. Travelling northwards through Mönchsroth, the route goes through pastoral countryside for 2km to Diederstetten, where the River Wörnitz is met for the first time since it was left just north of Harburg. Its course is closely followed all the way to Dinkelsbühl, where Mönchsrother Strasse leads through the southern suburbs to enter the historic walled town through the Nördlinger Tor.

Dinkelsbühl

The history of **DINKELSBÜHL** is remarkably similar to that of Nördlingen. It is believed to have been a Frankish royal seat as early as the 8th century, though it is first documented, under the name of Tinkelspuhel, in 1188, when Emperor Frederich Barbarossa bestowed it on his son Conrad as a wedding present. On the extinction of the Imperial Hohenstaufen dynasty, Dinkelsbühl passed to the Counts of Oettingen, who held it from 1251 until it gained the status of a Free Imperial City in 1341. It was already fortified with walls in the late 13th century, and these were extended and improved in the 1370s.

The Reformation split Dinkelsbühl into two camps. Although the Protestants were in the majority, a Catholic-only council was imposed on the town during the Schmalkaldic Wars of 1546. The duality of its religious make-up meant that Dinkelsbühl was a particular target during the Thirty Years' War, and it changed hands on no fewer than eight occasions. A peaceful coexistence of the two faiths was enshrined in a concordat signed after the end of the war, but the town never recovered its former prosperity. It did, however, subsequently acquire a few Baroque buildings, and is thus not so relentlessly medieval in appearance as Nördlingen. In 1802 it was incorporated by Bavaria, was taken over by Prussia in 1804, but returned permanently to Bavarian control in 1806. The town escaped damage in both World Wars, and now has a population of some 12,000.

Except for the loss of all but a small section of its sentry walk, the **Stadtmauer** (Town Wall) survives complete. A walk round its outer perimeter is especially rewarding, as the views are often enhanced by the presence of water: to the east, the Wörnitz and its channel, the Mühlgraben; to the north, the Gaulweiher (Nag's Head Pond).

The **Nördlinger Tor** (Nordlingen Gate), where the Romantic Road arrives from the south, dates back to the 14th century, except for the stepped gable, which was added around 1600. Adjoining it is one of Dinkelsbühl's most distinctive buildings, the **Stadtmühle** (Town Mill), which owes its existence to a decree issued by Emperor Charles IV, granting the town the right to have two mills. In order to harness the water of the Mühlgraben, it had to be built outside the existing Stadtmauer. Thus it was provided with its own fortified wall complete with sentry walk and firing positions; even the corner towers were designed primarily with defence in mind, and are equipped with cannon ports.

The Stadtmühle now houses the privately owned **Museum 3. Dimension**, an unexpected hi-tech addition to this medieval city's roster of sights. Billed as the first and as yet only museum of its kind in existence, its theme is the phenomenon of depth in all its manifestations. The displays are predominantly of the "hands-on" variety, encouraging visitors to conduct their own experiments. Among the subjects covered are rotating optical illusions, perspectives, holography, light polarization, prismatic screens, anaglyphs, stereoscopic cameras and photography, and 3-D art forms such as anamorphoses. Future plans include 3-D projections, television and computer games, and the installation of a camera obscura in the Nördlinger Tor.

Continuing round the Stadtmauer in an anticlockwise direction, there are particularly beautiful water-framed views over Dinkelsbühl's eastern skyline from the meadows on the island between the Wörnitz and the Mühlgraben. This stretch of wall is distinguished by another of the town's best-known landmarks, the **Bauerlinsturm**. Although named in honour of a municipal watchman who lived in the 15th century, it was not until later that the half-timbered upper storey was perched above the original stone tower to serve as a residence. Further north along the same stretch, the wall is defended by the **Henkersturm** (Hangman's

Dinkelsbühl, the Bauerlinsturm

Tower) and the **Dreigangsturm** (Three-part Tower).

The eastern entrance to the town is guarded by the **Wörnitz Tor** (Wörnitz Gate), so called because it stands beside the channel linking the Mühlgraben to the Wörnitz. It is the only one of the city's gates to date back to the original fortification system, though it was prettified around 1600 by the addition of a Renaissance gable.

From the Wörnitz Tor, a path travels alongside the north-eastern part of the walls through the Bleicher, a green used in former times by local weavers for bleaching their products. This leads to the **Rothenburger Tor** (Rothenburg Gate), the most formidable of the four gateways, itself guarded by a gatehouse equipped with firing positions. It was built around 1390 as the culmination of the programme to strengthen the original defences, but (like the Wörnitz Tor) was later embellished with a Renaissance gable. There is a particularly fine view from across the Gaulweiher, a carp pond much frequented by birds. At its far end, guarding the north-western corner of the Stadtmauer, is the circular **Faulturm**, which formerly served as a debtors' prison. Alongside is a pretty stone house with a half-timbered upper storey and steeply pitched roof.

The path continues via the bed of the drained moat to the cylindrical **Grüner Turm** (Green Tower), the tallest of the Stadtmauer's towers. It contrasts strikingly with the **Dreikönigstürmlein** (Little Tower of the Three Kings) beyond, which is built oddly out of line with the wall's course. Next comes the **Baroque Segringer Tor** (Segringen Gate), the western entrance to the town.

The Alte (Old) Promenade travels along the embankment opposite the final stretch of the Stadtmauer, the moat below it having been reclaimed to serve as allotments. This section is guarded by no fewer than eight towers. First in line are the **Wächtersturm** (Watchman's Tower), the **Berlinsturm** (which is named after a prominent family of medieval Dinkelsbühl, not the German capital), and the **Haymarsturm**.

These are followed by the **Weisser Turm** (White Tower), which is now linked to the promenade by a covered wooden bridge, and the **Hagelsturm** (Hail Tower). The ensemble is completed by a trio of round towers: the **Hertlesturm**, the **Krugsturm** (Jug Tower) and

View in the Tauber valley

Weikersheim, the Schloss, with the Stadtkirche in the background

Würzburg, the Festung Marienberg and the church of St Burkard viewed from across the Main

the **Königsturm** (King's Tower). From the end of the promenade, there is an excellent vista back to the last five towers, whose appearance from this angle well justifies their nickname, the Turmparade ("Parade of Towers").

Arriving back at the Nördlinger Tor, it is a short walk straight ahead along Nördlinger Strasse to the town centre. At the end of the street is the **Paulskirche** (St Paul's Church), a plain preaching hall built in 1840 on the site of a former Carmelite monastery to serve as a new place of worship for the local Protestant community.

Down to the right are two adjoining squares, the Ledermarkt (Leather Market) and the Altrathausplatz. The latter, one of Dinkelsbühl's most picturesque corners, is framed to the east by the Wörnitz Tor. It takes its name from the **Altes Rathaus** (Old Town Hall), which was built in the 14th century as a private patrician residence, and extended and rebuilt on several subsequent occasions. In the middle of the square is the 16th century **Löwenbrunnen** (Lion Fountain), whose central column features a seated lion bearing the municipal coat-of-arms. At no. 12 on the square is the **Kunssberghaus**, whose garden gives access to the sole surviving section of the Stadtmauer's sentry walk.

Rising up behind the opposite side of the square is the town's single most dominant landmark, the **Georgskirche** (St George's Church). This is rightly regarded as one of the purest and most beautiful of all Germany's Gothic hall churches, although the tower is something of an anomaly. Built around 1225 as the detached belfry of the previous Romanesque church, it was only incorporated into the new design because a shortage of funds precluded its replacement. Its off-centre position on the facade, where it is flanked by differently sized gables, is eccentric but effective, and the bell chamber and domed octagon added in the mid-16th century give it at least a partially Gothic character. In summer, it is usually possible to ascend to the balcony, which commands a wonderful view over Dinkelsbühl and the surrounding countryside.

Facing the north side of the church across the spacious Weinmarkt (Wine Market) are five splendidly gabled buildings, all erected around 1600. First in line, on the corner with Senglinger Strasse, is the **Ratsherrnstube** (Town Councillors' Tavern), which nowadays houses municipal offices, a library and the tourist office. The middle building, an outstanding example of Renaissance half-timbering, is

Dinkelsbühl's best-known hotel, the **Deutsches Haus**. At the end of the row is the **Schranne**, which was built for threshing and storing corn, but is now the town's main festive hall.

Dr-Martin-Luther-Strasse, which links the Weinmarkt with the Rothenburger Tor, is dominated by the extensive complex of the **Spital zum Heiligen Geist** (Hospital of the Holy Ghost) on its south side. The oldest surviving part is the chapel, which dates back to around 1380, though its interior was remodelled in Baroque style in the 18th century, when the galleries were added. A half-timbered building in the courtyard houses the **Historisches Museum** (Historical Museum), whose exhibits include topographical views of Dinkelsbühl, municipal treasury items, souvenirs of the local guilds, weapons, torture instruments, historic toys and a complete 19th century apothecary.

From the western end of the Weinmarkt, Segringer Strasse leads uphill to the Segringer Tor. It is lined with some notable mansions, in particular nos. 3 and 5, which share a single gable, and the **Hezelhof** at no. 7, which has an idyllic flower-strewn inner courtyard. Further up, on the opposite side of the street, is the Baroque **Neues Rathaus** (New Town Hall), which was built in 1733 as the private residence of a prosperous citizen who later became mayor. At the top end of the street is the **Dreikönigskapelle** (Chapel of the Three Kings), a 14th century foundation of the Berlin family which has served since 1922 as a war memorial.

Kapuzinerweg leads north from the Segringer Tor along the inner perimeter of the Stadtmauer, past the former **Kapuzinerkloster** (Capuchin Monastery) and a Baroque wayside shrine with a sculptural representation of the Crucifixion. From there, Obere Schmiedgasse leads back down to Dr-Martin-Luther-Strasse. Walking in the opposite direction from the Segringer Tor, Oberer Mauerweg leads all the way along the inner side of the Stadtmauer to the Nördlinger Tor.

En route, it is well worth making a detour down to see the monumental Baroque complex of the **Deutschordenshaus** (House of the Teutonic Knights) on Turmgasse, and in particular the tiny Rococo chapel on the top floor of its west wing. The tour of the accessible parts of the inner wall is completed by following Unterer Mauerweg north from the Nördlinger Tor past the Bauerlinsturm to the Dreigangsturm.

STAGE 16:
DINKELSBÜHL TO FEUCHTWANGEN (13km)

The stage between Dinkelsbühl and Feuchtwangen is among the least eventful on the Romantic Road, passing as it does through the rather monotonous agricultural land of the Frankenhöhe plain, with no notable historic sights en route.

Leaving Dinkelsbühl by the Rothenburger Tor, the northern outskirts are soon left behind as the route travels along tracks and minor roads on the left bank of the River Wörnitz. After 5km, the village of Burgstall can be seen to the west, but is bypassed completely, as is the market town of Schopfloch, which can be seen to the right 2km further on.

Not until Larrieden, another 1.5km to the north, does the route enter a human settlement. Here it turns right to cross the Wörnitz, then left at a junction, continuing slightly uphill through pastoral land for 2km to the hamlet of Heiligenkreuz. From there, it goes downhill along the side of a wood for 2.5km to Kaltenbronn, a scattered farming community surrounded by ponds. At the western end of the village, it bears left to follow a path through the fields which runs along the side of the rail line.

After a further 2.5km, it arrives at **FEUCHTWANGEN**, a town with a marginally larger population than Dinkelsbühl's.

Feuchtwangen
Feuchtwangen grew from a Benedictine monastery established around the turn of the 9th century by Emperor Charlemagne. In 1241, it became a Free Imperial City, but lost this status in 1376 when Emperor Charles IV sold it to the ambitious Hohenzollern dynasty (the ancestors of the Kaisers of the Second Reich), who incorporated it into the Burgraviate of Nuremberg. This territory was partitioned in 1403, and Feuchtwangen became part of the new Margraviate of Brandenburg-Ansbach, which survived on the map until its annexation by Bavaria in 1806.

The route enters Feuchtwangen from the west, crossing over the rail tracks to reach Ringstrasse, then following Untere Torstrasse

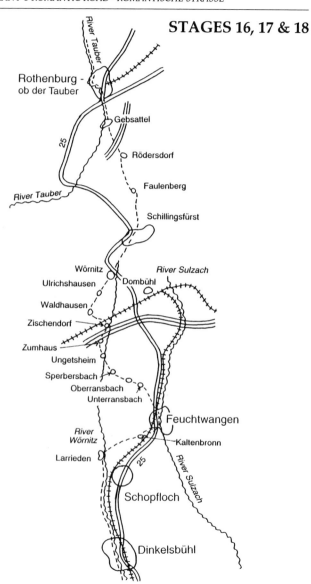

STAGES 16, 17 & 18

River Tauber

Rothenburg - ob der Tauber

Gebsattel

Rödersdorf

Faulenberg

Schillingsfürst

River Tauber

25

Wörnitz

River Sulzach

Ulrichshausen

Dombühl

Waldhausen

Zischendorf

Zumhaus

Ungetsheim

Sperbersbach

Oberransbach

Unterransbach

Feuchtwangen

Kaltenbronn

River Wörnitz

Larrieden

25

River Sulzach

Schopfloch

Dinkelsbühl

uphill. At the top of the street is the **Schranne**, whose passageway houses a collection of old firefighting equipment. Directly opposite, facing on to Marktplatz, is the Baroque **Neues Rathaus** (New Town Hall). Also on the square are a number of half-timbered mansions and **Röhrenbrunnen**, a fountain bearing a column statue of Minerva.

Backing on to the south-west corner Marktplatz is the **Stiftskirche** (Collegiate Church), founded around 1150 as the successor to the Benedictine monastery which previously occupied the site. Of the original Romanesque church, the twin-towered facade survives, albeit in a much altered form; the rest of the structure was completely rebuilt in Gothic style. When the college was suppressed following the adoption of the Reformation in Brandenburg-Ansbach, the Stiftskirche became a Protestant parish church. In 1698, the interior was remodelled according to Lutheran tenets, gaining side galleries, a new pulpit and organ. However, some pre-Reformation furnishings were retained. These include the high altar, which was made in 1484 in the workshop of Dürer's teacher, the Nuremberg master Michael Wolgemut; and the vigorously carved choir stalls from around 1500.

On the south side of the Stiftskirche is another Romanesque survivor, the **Kreuzgang** (Cloisters). Open-air theatrical performances, which are rated Feuchtwangen's biggest tourist draw, are held in this romantically semi-ruinous setting each summer. The west wing houses the **Handwerkstuben** (Handcraft Workshops), which has six reassembled historic work rooms - of a confectioner, a weaver, a cobbler, a dyer, a potter and a pewterer.

Facing the northern side of the Stiftskirche is the much smaller **Johanniskirche** (St John's Church). Its origins are obscure, but in its present form it dates back to 1414. Prior to the Reformation, it served as a parish church; afterwards, it was used as a baptistery. The vault paintings, tabernacle, font and pulpit all date from the 15th century, the altar from 1680. Alongside is a building known as the **Kasten** (literally, "Box"), which was built in 1565 as a tithe barn, and now serves as a hall for concerts and receptions.

Museumstrasse leads from the north-eastern corner of Marktplatz to the **Fränkisches Museum** (Franconian Museum), which is devoted to the folk culture of the region. The changing tastes of bourgeois and farming households over the past two centuries are illustrated in a series of fully furnished interiors in styles ranging from Baroque to Jugendstil. Other highlights are the collection of faience produced in Franconian factories, and the small open-air section in the back yard, featuring a barn and a smithy.

STAGE 17:
FEUCHTWANGEN TO SCHILLINGSFÜRST (20km)
(See map p132)

The way out of Feuchtwangen lies by returning to Ringstrasse, and continuing straight ahead by the path alongside the B25. After 1km, the route leaves the main road, turning left to skirt the hamlet of Weil am See, from where it follows the Ransbach stream to the adjacent villages of Unterransbach and Oberransbach. In the latter, where there is a very rare example of ambiguous waymarking, it is necessary to go right the way up to the highest houses in the village, and then to continue ascending into the woods beyond.

A forest track then follows a snaking course for about 1km, before emerging to descend through the fields to Sperbersbach, which lies back in the valley of the Wörnitz. Bearing westwards through the village, the route turns right at the end to go north for a short distance along the right bank of the river, before turning left over the bridge, then right into Ungetsheim. It goes northwards through the village, before passing under the A6/E50 motorway.

On the other side is **ZUMHAUS**, which is 9km from Feuchtwangen, albeit still part of its municipal area. *This tiny village is a favourite rendezvous point for cyclists, particularly those travelling the Romantic Road, as house no. 4 contains the **Fahrradmuseum** (Bicycle Museum). The first of its type in the whole of Southern Germany, it exhibits over 100 historic bikes, most of them unrestored, which document the technical developments that have occurred over the past two centuries. For those tempted to linger, there is a shady beer garden outside, as well as basic camping facilities.*

At a T-junction in the centre of Zumhaus, the route turns right and crosses over the Wörnitz once again, then turns left and travels towards Zischendorf, 1km to the north. Here there is another T-junction, and again a left turn is made. The way ahead lies through the tunnel under the Crailsheim to Ansbach railway, then on to Waldhausen and Ulrichshausen. At the edge of the latter, the route turns left then right, and continues on to Wörnitz, whose name derives from its proximity to the source of the eponymous river. At the northern end of the village, which is 6km on from Zumhaus, the route travels under the B25. A short distance beyond is Riedenberg, where it turns first to the right and then to the left and proceeds northwards to Wittumö.

From there, it follows the road which loops round via the Frankenhohe campsite to reach **SCHILLINGSFÜRST**, which is some 5km from Wörnitz.

Schillingsfürst

This little town, whose population even today numbers less than 2,500, has for centuries been one of the seats of the House of Hohenlohe, a dynasty which established feudal control over large tracts of rural Franconia in the early Middle Ages and still owns substantial holdings there, including a dozen stately homes.

The family split into Catholic and Protestant lines in 1553, and when the territory of the former was itself divided in 1744, Schillingsfürst became the capital of a tiny new principality, Hohenlohe-Schillingsfürst. This came to unlikely prominence in the latter part of the 19th century, when the ruling Prince Chlodwig, whose younger brother served as a cardinal in Rome, rose to become one of the most eminent statesmen of the Second German Reich. In 1894, at the age of 75, he was appointed by Kaiser Wilhelm II to Bismarck's old offices of Imperial Chancellor of Germany and Minister-President of Prussia, holding both posts until his retirement in 1900. The period saw a marked shift in Germany's foreign policy, with the British Empire increasingly regarded as a rival, rather than the natural ally it had hitherto been.

At the end of Dombühler Strasse, which runs from the campsite to the southern outskirts of town, a right turn leads into Frankenheimer Strasse, at the end of which is the main square, Am Markt. A short distance east along Hohenlohestrasse are the Steinerne Steige ("Stone Steps"), which lead up to the **Schloss** perched atop the wooded hill above, dominating the Frankenhöhe plain for miles around. The present residential palace is the successor to various fortified castles which have occupied the spot since the year 1000. It was built between 1723 and 1750 for Prince Philipp Ernst, the founder of the Hohenlohe-Schillingsfürst line. The Schloss is still lived in by the family, though a few of the main rooms can be visited by guided tour. These feature stuccowork and ceiling paintings from the initial construction period, as well as period furnishings and mementoes of Prince Chlodwig.

As a tourist attraction, the Schloss is overshadowed by the **Bayrischer Jagdfalkenhof** (Bavarian Falconry) in its grounds. This is home to a large number of birds of prey, including eagles, falcons, buzzards, hawks, vultures and owls, and throughout the day most of these can be seen chained to posts outside their enclosures. Professional falconers conduct demonstrations of some of the birds in free flight at 11am and 3pm daily between March and October, and additionally at 5pm from May to August.

Outside the built-up part of Schillingsfürst, about 1.5km due east of the Schloss via Am Wall, Neue Gasse and Brunnenhausweg, is the **Brunnenhaus** (Well-House). This shelters one of the most remarkable technical monuments in Germany, the Ochsentret-scheibenpumpwerk ("Ox's Treadmill Pump"), which was built in 1702. Its sloping wooden turntable was rotated by the walking movements of an ox, thereby activating the iron crankshaft connected with rods to three pumps which brought water up from the well. The water was then channelled through a system of wooden conduits to the Schloss.

SCHILLINGSFÜRST TO ROTHENBURG OB DER TAUBER (18km)
(See map p132)

From Schillingfürst's Markt, the route begins by turning north into Rothenburger Strasse. However, it does not continue out of town along the main road to Rothenburg; instead it follows a series of minor roads through farming country which as yet have little in the way of special tracks for cyclists and walkers. At the first fork it bears right along Am Haag, which curves round below the Schloss then twists uphill and downhill for the 2km to Wohnbach, continuing on for a further 1km to Neuweiler. At the edge of this village, the route turns sharp left and travels east for 2km to Faulenberg. Here there is an austere Pfarrkirche (Parish Church) which is Romanesque in origin, though its character was later modified by the addition of tall Gothic windows.

At the western end of Faulenberg, the route turns right and travels alongside then through wooded countryside, before descending to Rodersdorf, 3km on. Bearing left at the end of the village, it crosses the flyover on the A7/E43 motorway, from where there is an absolutely breathtaking distant view of Rothenburg ob der Tauber, imperiously perched on its heights, and mantled with towers and battlements.

The route continues downhill for a further 2km to Gebstattel, which lies on the banks of the Tauber, whose course is closely followed for the next 80km of the Romantic Road. Initially, however, the route travels some way back from the river, which first comes into view midway between Gebstattel and St Leonhard, the next village to the north.

It is then 2km to the southern outskirts of Rothenburg, which can be reached by several different routes. The most direct way is to follow the main road, Nördlinger Strasse, straight ahead, but it is far preferable to bear leftwards along Taubertalweg from the centre of St Leonhard. This goes along the side of the Tauber, crossing from the right to the left bank at one of the valley's many mills, the Walkmühle. The route continues onwards past the Schmelzmühle, crosses over the Schandtauber stream at the point where it flows into the Tauber, and continues on to the Gipsmühle.

At this point there is the option of crossing back to the right bank, then continuing northwards via a woodland path, which emerges just below the Spitalbastei, the southern entrance to the historic part of Rothenburg. Alternatively, there is the option of proceeding onwards along the left bank from the Gipsmühle, and crossing over at the next bridge. It is then necessary to follow the main road to the town centre northwards for a short distance, then to turn right up a steep path which enters Rothenburg at the Kobolzeller Tor.

Rothenburg ob der Tauber

ROTHENBURG OB DER TAUBER perfectly encapsulates the Romantic image of medieval Germany. There is not a single obviously modern intruder in its immaculately preserved and maintained townscape of Gothic and Renaissance buildings, which occupies a truly spectacular natural setting on a promontory some 90m above the River Tauber. It is by far the most famous and most visited small town in the country, one that has gained the status of an essential stop on any modern-day grand tour of Europe.

Although Celtic tribes are known to have established a fortified settlement on the opposite side of the Tauber around 500BC, the site of Rothenburg does not appear to have been inhabited until a local nobleman, Count Reigner, established a feudal stronghold there around 970. When his descendants died out in 1106, Rothenburg passed into the hands of the Imperial Hohenstaufen dynasty, and was bestowed on the future Emperor Conrad III, in whose reign it became a favourite seat of the German court.

This role was not maintained under subsequent emperors, but nonetheless the town continued to grow in importance. It gained a charter in 1172 and soon afterwards was enclosed within a set of walls. However, expansion continued at such a rate that by 1204 it was already necessary to build new fortifications, which increased the length of wall from 1.4km to 2.4km. Rothenburg gained the status of a Free Imperial City in 1274, and between 1350 and 1380

*Rothenburg ob der Tauber, the Reichstadtfest: tableau of a
19th century church fair*

expanded to the south, necessitating the construction of a further
1km of wall. As a result, the town assumed a highly distinctive
shape, which has been compared both to a wine glass and to a
question mark, with the newest section serving as the stalk.

At the turn of the 15th century, under the rule of Burgomaster
Heinrich Toppler, Rothenburg ranked among the richest city-states
in Germany, one whose jurisdiction covered 167 outlying villages
spread over some 400sq km. The municipality had a total population
of around 20,000 (the present-day figure, in a much smaller municipal
area, is 13,000), nearly a third of whom lived in the town itself.
Toppler's involvement in the conspiracy to reinstate the deposed
King Wenzel resulted not only in his own imprisonment and death
in mysterious circumstances, but also to a loss of status for
Rothenburg. Over the next century and a half the city suffered many
vicissitudes, particularly during the struggles of the Reformation
period, where it was a staunch backer of Protestantism. It recovered
to enjoy another period of great prosperity during the last three
decades of the 16th century, when the municipal architect Leonhard

Weidmann embellished it with some of the finest buildings of the German Renaissance.

Nowadays, the Thirty Years' War is celebrated in myth as a heroic era in Rothenburg's history. The reality is that the defences proved hopelessly outdated, and the city was repeatedly occupied and plundered. By the end of the war, it was left heavily in debt, with its population reduced by half, and it thereafter sank into provincial obscurity. It was not until long after its incorporation into Bavaria in 1802 that it recovered some prestige as a result of its "rediscovery" by the poets and painters of the Romantic movement, who were infatuated with all things medieval.

In 1945, Rothenburg was the victim of an aerial bombardment carried out by American forces, sustaining a fair amount of damage in the process. Thankfully, the exercise was not repeated, due to the prompt action of J.J. McCloy, the future US High Commissioner to Germany, who knew and loved the city and successfully lobbied for it to be spared from further bombing. Rothenburg was faithfully restored after the war, thanks in no small measure to foreign help. Tourism is now the mainstay of the local economy, providing employment for nearly half the working population. It is underpinned by the strictest conservation policies in Germany, which go as far as enforcing even the biggest international chains to use traditional wrought-iron shop signs instead of corporate logos.

At the heart of the town is the sloping Marktplatz, one of the country's most imposing market squares. On its north side stands the **Ratsherrentrinkstube** (Councillors' Tavern), a Gothic building of 1446 which now houses the tourist office. Its gabled front is decorated with a sundial from 1768, a carving of the Imperial double eagle with the coat-of-arms of Rothenburg, and two clocks, one from 1683, the other from 1910. On either side of the latter are shutters which open every hour between 11am and 3pm and 8pm and 10pm to reveal figures which enact the most famous legend associated with Rothenburg.

This apocryphal event supposedly occurred on 31st October 1631, when the city was captured by the Imperial army commanded by Count Johann Tilly, a Catholic stalwart with a reputation for carrying out brutal acts of retribution against defeated Protestant foes. Fearing that Rothenburg would be laid waste, the townsfolk gathered in the Marktplatz to plead for mercy. As a peace-offering Tilly was offered a drink from the huge municipal tankard, which was filled to capacity with 3$^1/_4$ litres of wine. Being a teetotaller, he refused this, but was humoured enough to promise to spare the town if one of the councillors could empty the contents in a single draught. The former burgomaster Georg Nusch accepted the wager and, to the astonishment of everyone, duly accomplished the feat in ten minutes. He needed three days to sleep off the effects, but suffered no long-term damage to his health.

The whole of the west side of Marktplatz is occupied by the **Rathaus** (Town Hall), which falls into two clearly defined parts. To the rear is the surviving half of the original Gothic Rathaus, which was erected between 1250 and 1400. The rest of this was destroyed by fire in 1501, and replaced in 1572-8 with a new Renaissance building by Leonhard Weidmann. This is not only a remarkable composition in its own right, in which the central stair turret and the corner oriels dramatically interrupt the otherwise severely linear design; it also dovetails quite perfectly with the older structure, whose slender 60m high tower retains a position of pre-eminence.

Access to both parts of the building is via the stair turret, which leads up to a spacious landing hung with coats-of-arms of prominent local families as well as a portrait of Heinrich Toppler in armour. Beyond is the Kaisersaal (Imperial Hall), a splendid wood-beamed Gothic chamber remodelled by Weidmann. Several times each year, it hosts performances of *Der Meistertrunk (The Master Draught)*, a costumed drama by Adam Hörber, a local craftsman, who wrote it to celebrate the 250th anniversary of the legendary episode of 1631. Plays by Hans Sachs, the celebrated 16th century cobbler-poet of Nuremberg, are also regularly performed there.

On the second floor landing are coats-of-arms of Rothenburg, the Holy Roman Empire and the seven Electors, as well as Weidmann's own monogram. From there, a narrow staircase leads up to the top of the tower, which commands a magnificent bird's-eye view over Rothenburg and the Tauber valley. Although there are many fine vantage points in the town, this is the only one readily accessible to visitors which clearly reveals its highly distinctive shape.

The inner courtyard between the Gothic and Renaissance parts of the Rathaus is entered via a portal on either side of which are the measurements used in Rothenburg's period as a city state: the Rute or rod (3.93m), the Schuh or foot (30cm), the Elle or yard (59cm) and the Klafter or fathom (1.93m). A splendid Renaissance portal within the courtyard gives access to the **Historiengewölbe** (Historical Vaults). The ground floor is laid out as a series of tableaux depicting events around the time of the Thirty Years' War; among the scenes are the Meistertrunk legend and the laboratory of the alchemist Andreas Libvarius. In the basement are the guard room, the torture chamber and the prison cells where Heinrich Toppler was incarcerated in 1408, dying there three months later.

The colourful **Georgsbrunnen** (St George's Fountain) on the south side of Marktplatz dates back to 1446 but did not assume its present appearance until 1608. It is some 8m deep and was capable of storing an emergency reserve of 100,000 litres of water. Beside it stand two fine examples of half-timbering. The **Fleisch- und Tanzhaus** (Meat and Dance House) is so called because of its curious dual role: the ground floor, which nowadays contains a gallery of paintings by local artists, originally served as a butchers' market, while the first floor was the municipal dance hall. A pharmacy now occupies the **Jagstheimerhaus** alongside, a mansion with a picturesque corner oriel which takes its name from the 15th century burgomaster who commissioned it.

Down Hofbronnengasse, the alley immediately to the south, is the privately owned **Puppen- und Spielzeug Museum** (Doll and Toy Museum), which features several hundred items from the period 1780 to 1940. In addition to individual dolls and toys made from wood, wax, papier mâché, rags, porcelain and celluloid, there are many more elaborate exhibits, including dolls' houses, dolls' shops, puppet theatres, carousels and train sets.

Herrngasse, which leads west from Marktplatz, is the widest street in Rothenburg, and itself the setting for occasional markets, which are held around the **Herrnbrunnen** (Gentlemen's Fountain). Traditionally the home of the town's patrician class, Herrngasse is lined with a series of handsome gabled mansions equipped with pulleys for hoisting goods up from the street. Rothenburg's most prestigious hotel, the Eisenhut, occupies four of these houses, though others are still private residences. These include the

Staudtsches Haus at no. 18, where visitors can ring the doorbell for a short guided tour which takes in the lobby, the kitchen, the remarkable wooden stairwell and the galleried courtyard.

Opposite is the **Franziskanerkirche** (Franciscan Church), built between 1281 and 1308 in the austere Gothic style favoured by the mendicant orders of friars. Although the adjoining monastery was pulled down when Rothenburg adopted the Reformation, the church itself is well preserved.

At the far end of Herrngasse is the charming little **Figurentheater** (Puppet Theatre), which has attracted international acclaim for the gentle humour and artistic integrity of its shows, which normally use a mixture of German and English. It stands directly in the lee of the 14th century **Burgtor** (Castle Gate), the tallest of the town's gateways. The original construction received a number of embellishments in the 16th century, including an outer gate with paired guardhouses, and the Nadelohr (eye of a needle), a passageway which enabled the sentries to allow individuals to enter without having to raise the drawbridge.

Beyond is the shady **Burggarten** (Castle Garden), which offers immaculately tended flower beds and wonderful views across to the south-western part of the town's skyline and down into the Tauber valley. It occupies the site of the original feudal castle from which Rothenburg developed, as well as the later imperial castle, both of which were destroyed in an earthquake in 1356. Around 1400, Heinrich Toppler had the surviving masonry reused in the construction of the **Blasiuskapelle** (St Blase's Chapel), which now serves as a memorial to those who lost their lives in the two World Wars.

A block north of Marktplatz is the town's most prominent landmark, the Gothic church of **St Jakob** (St James). This adopts the idiosyncratic German format of having choirs at both ends of the building, and rises like a great ship above the sea of red roofs all around. It was constructed at a leisurely pace between 1311 and 1484, beginning with the east choir and ending with the elevated west choir, which is built above an archway straddling the street. The two towers are of slightly different height (55m and 58m) and design. According to legend, the northern tower, which is higher and crowned by a more elaborate openwork spire, was the work of the apprentice of the master mason who built the southern tower. So overcome was the master with jealousy that he committed suicide.

The church's most valuable treasure is the great Heilig-Blut-Altar (Holy Blood Altar) by Tilman Riemenschneider in the west choir. It's main scene of the last supper, which is carved in the round, adopts the boldly dramatic device of making Judas Iscariot the central character: the relief carvings on the wings depict two more Passion scenes, the Entry into Jerusalem and the Agony in the Garden of Gethsemane. The altar was specially commissioned as a shrine for the church's most precious relic, a rock crystal containing three drop's of Chirst blood, which is displayed inside the gilded cross above the main scene.

Immediately to the north of St Jakob is the former **Gymnasium** (Grammar School), which is nowadays a community centre. Built in Renaissance style in 1589 by Leonhard Weidmann, it has an octagonal staircase tower with sundial, and was later adorned with an elaborate Baroque portal. On Klingengasse, the alley leading northwards from the archway under the church, is another fine Renaissance building, the half-timbered **Feuerlinshaus**, which has a charming oriel window.

On Klosterhof, a few paces down to the left, is the former **Dominikanerinnenkloster** (Dominican Convent). Although its church was demolished in 1813, this early Gothic complex still ranks among Rothenburg's most distinguished buildings, one which makes a fitting home for the excellent local history collections of the **Reichstadtmuseum** (Imperial City Museum). Of special note is the Klosterküche, the oldest surviving kitchen in Germany. It dates back to 1258, and still preserves many medieval features, including the huge fireplace which was the only significant source of heat in the entire convent.

An old barn at the northern end of Klingengasse has been converted to house the **Bauerliches Museum** (Farming Museum), which displays historic farming tools and machinery from all over Franconia. The street is closed off by the late 14th century **Klingentor** (Klingen Gate), whose tower, with its graceful little corner turrets, was formerly used for water storage. It was later strengthened by the addition of a bastion to the north.

Alongside is the towerless late Gothic church of **St Wolfgang**, which was built between 1475 and 1492 and formerly served as the parish of the local shepherds. Its austere northern wall, pierced only by embrasures, formed part of the municipal fortifications and is therefore decidedly unecclesiastical in appearance; the southern facade, in contrast, is highly picturesque. Inside, there are three altars dating from just after the church's construction. It is also possible to descend to the casemates below the church, with their dungeons and gun emplacements, and to ascend to the sentry's house above the adjoining gateway. Within the latter is a permanent exhibition on the Schäfertanz (Shepherds' Dance), which is performed on the Marktplatz on selected Sundays in summer. According to one tradition, the dance began as a thanksgiving for Rothenburg's deliverance from the plague; another theory asserts that it derives from a shepherd's discovery of hidden treasure.

Returning a short distance back along Klingengasse, Judengasse leads west to the **Weisser Turm** (White Tower), one of the surviving parts of the 12th century fortifications. Beside it is the half-timbered **Judentanzhaus** (Jewish Dance House), which displays Jewish gravestones on its garden wall. A couple of blocks to the south, separating Hafengasse and Rodergasse, are the only other surviving parts of the original town wall: the hip-roofed **Markusturm** (St Mark's Tower) and the **Röderbogen** (Roder Arch), to which a clock turret was later appended. Adjoining the former is the **Buttelhaus** (Bailiff's House), whose barred windows indicate its former function as the town prison.

A few paces to the south, at Alter Stadtgraben 27, is the **Alt-Rothenburger Handwerkerhaus** (Old Rothenburg Craftsmen's House). Dating back to 1270, this is believed to be the oldest surviving house in the town. Its eleven rooms have been furnished in the style of centuries past, features of special note include the kitchen with its stone hearth and open fireplace, the tiled stove in the living room, and the well, which reaches to a depth of 14m.

Some of the finest mansions in town can be seen on Schmiedgasse, which leads off the south-east corner of Marktplatz. The **Baumeisterhaus** (Architects' House), nowadays a leading café-restaurant, is named in honour of Leonhard Weidmann, who built it in 1596. Its first floor is adorned with statues of the Seven Cardinal

Virtues; on the next level, the Seven Deadly Sins sound their warning notes. Inside is a quaint half-timbered courtyard with two tiers of galleries. Further down the street, an inn called the Roter Hahn occupies the mansion of Burgomaster Nusch of Meistertrunk fame.

Opposite the latter is the **Johanniskirche** (St John's Church). Nowadays the Catholic parish church, it was built between 1390 and 1410 as part of a commandery of the Order of St John. The Baroque monastic buildings alongside house the fascinatingly offbeat **Mittelalteriches Kriminalmuseum** (Medieval Crime Museum), which is labelled throughout in English as well as German. In the courtyard is a wooden cage used for ducking bakers who produced undersized loaves; indoors are examples of many other crude devices of punishment and torture, from the beer barrels drunks were forced to walk around in to the nail-encrusted chairs used during witchcraft trials. There is also extensive documentation on many aspects of law and justice, including a host of amusing caricatures.

Towards the lower end of Schmiedgasse is the Plönlein, an irresistibly photogenic triangular square formed by a fork in the road. Ahead is the **Siebersturm** (Siebers Tower), which was formerly the southern entrance to the town; the alley to the right leads down to the **Kobolzeller Tor** (Kobolzell Gate), a mighty double gateway with a look-out point known as the Teufelkanzel (Devil's Pulpit).

Beyond the Siebersturm is the Spitalviertel (Hospital Quarter), which lay outside the walls prior to the final expansion of the medieval town in the 14th century. The town's youth hostel occupies the huge **Rossmühle** (Horse Mill) at the western edge of the district, which was built in 1516 to provide emergency cover for occasions when the mills in the valley below were cut off during a siege. It had four grinding wheels, which were worked by sixteen horses. Further south adjoining the **Stöberleinsturm**, a 14th century tower with dainty little corner turrets, is a late 17th century tithe barn, which in 1975 was converted into the **Reichstadthalle** (Imperial City Hall), a venue for congresses and other special events.

The **Heilig-Geist-Spital** (Holy Ghost Hospital) itself was founded in 1280, though of the original Gothic buildings only the **Spitalkirche** (Hospital Church) has survived. Leonhard Weidmann built both the main hospital block and the **Hegereiterhaus**, the elegant courtyard building with a tent-shaped roof and a cylindrical stair turret which served as the residence of the estate's administrator. The same architect was also involved in the construction of the **Spitalbastei** (Hospital Bastion), the strongest and most modern part of the entire defensive system, which is shaped like a figure-of-eight, with two inner courtyards and no fewer than seven gates.

As in Nördlingen, there are three ways of walking round the **Stadtmauer** (Town Wall) - around the inner and outer perimeters, and along the covered **Wehrgang** (sentry walk). To see the fortifications themselves to best effect, it is necessary to walk round the outer perimeter, though it has to be said that the sentry walk is by far the most enticing of the three circuits, as it offers a wonderful series of views over the town. Unfortunately, a substantial section is missing, but it can nevertheless be followed all the way from the Kobolzeller Tor to the Klingentor, a distance of 2.5km.

Starting at the former, it proceeds southwards via the Fischturm (Fish Tower), the Kalkturm (Chalk Tower), the Stöberleinsturm and the Sauturn (Sow Tower) to the Spitalbastei. It continues all the way along the eastern fringe of the town past the Kleiner Stern ("Little Star"), Grosser Stern ("Big Star"), the Faulturm, the Schwefelturm (Sulphur Tower) and the Hohennersturm to the **Rödertor** (Roder Gate), which is protected by a double bastion. The main tower can be ascended for an excellent view over the town; at the top there is also a small exhibition of photographs showing the bomb damage of 1945.

The sentry walk continues onwards past the Weiberturm (Weavers' Tower) and Thomasturm (Thomas Tower) to the **Würzburger Tor** (Würzburg Gate), the weakest part of the fortifications, and the place from which Tilly's forces entered the town in 1631. Public executions were formerly held outside, hence its alternative name of Galgentor (Gallows Gate). Next in line is the Ganserturm at the north-east corner, whose outlying bastion is nicknamed Kummereck ("Worry Corner") because of its vulnerability. There then follow the Henkersturm (Hangman's Tower) and the Pulverturm (Powder Tower) prior to the Klingertor, where the sentry walk now terminates.

To see the western section of the Stadtmauer, it is best to

Rothenburg ob der Tauber, view from the Rödertor

continue along the inner perimeter to the Strafturm (Punishment Tower), then to pass through the wall to follow the path along the outer perimeter past the Klosterturm (Convent Tower) and the Bettelvogtsturm to the Burggarten. From there, the path which runs eastwards from just below the Blasiuskapelle offers the best views of the remaining part of the Stadtmauer, which stands above a sheer drop. The two surviving towers along this stretch are the Fürbringerturm at the edge of the Burggarten, and the Johanniterturm (St John's Commandery Tower) beside the Mittelalteriches Kriminalmuseum.

This same pathway descends to the **Doppelbrücke** (Double Bridge), a 14th century viaduct faithfully reconstructed after World War II, which can be reached more directly by the much steeper path from the Kobolzeller Tor. From the bridge, there is a really magnificent long-range view of Rothenburg. More fine panoramas can be had from the road which follows the S-bend in the Tauber round to the **Topplerschlösschen**, a late 14th century tower-house built as a summer and weekend retreat for Burgomaster Topler. It has a bizarre top-heavy effect, with the upper storeys jutting out

149

Rothenburg ob der Tauber, the Doppelbrücke with a distant view of the town

well over the stumpy base.

From the covered wooden bridge just to the north, a path leads back up to the Burggarten. Alternatively, continue along the left bank of the river to the road bridge beyond, and cross over to the other side to pick up the official northbound route of the Romantic Road.

ROTHENBURG OB DER TAUBER TO CREGLINGEN
(20km)

Between Rothenburg and Tauberbischofsheim, the last staging-post before the terminus of Würzburg, the Romantic Road travels along the valley of the Tauber. It seldom strays very far from the riverbank, and follows exactly the same course as another well-established touring route known as the Liebliches Taubertal ("Lovely Tauber Valley"). This is undoubtedly one of the most delightful parts of the whole journey, not least because tracks designed solely for the use of cyclists and walkers cover this entire section without interruption. Moreover, the distances between each of the staging-posts are always short, there are interesting places in between, and the scenery is almost unremittingly attractive.

So grand is the valley of the still-young Tauber at Rothenburg that it might be expected that it would quickly assume the dimensions of a major river. In fact, it does not broaden out fully until shortly before its confluence with the Main at Wertheim. For most of its length, including the entire stretch where the Romantic Road runs alongside, it usually appears as little more than a stream, albeit an exceptionally pretty one. Its waters, and those of its tributaries, are pure and clear, and abundantly stocked with trout, eel, perch, pike and carp. The surrounding countryside is a fertile wine-producing area, but is also quite heavily wooded, the Tauber itself being almost constantly tree-lined. Due to the preponderance of deciduous species, it looks particularly beguiling in autumn.

The easiest way to leave Rothenburg is via the gate at the eastern end of the Burggarten, from where a path wends steeply downhill to the valley floor, and continues along the right bank of the Tauber to **DETWANG**, just under 2km away. *This red-roofed village is actually much older than Rothenburg, dating back at least as far as the 10th century. However, it was soon eclipsed by its neighbour, first coming* *under its jurisdiction at some point in the last quarter of the 13th century, and it remains part of the Rothenburg municipality to this day.*

*The church of **St Peter und Paul** (SS Peter and Paul), built in Romanesque style in the second half of the 12th century, is the oldest surviving place of worship in the Tauber valley. It subsequently received a number of Gothic alterations, including the replacement of the original east end with a new oratory (itself later converted into an ossuary) for the nuns who lived in the adjoining convent. As a result, the room below the tower has to serve as the chancel. This houses the celebrated Crucifixion triptych by Tilman Riemenschneider, carved in 1510 for a now vanished cemetery chapel in Rothenburg, The central panel of the Crucifixion is a sensitive original composition by the master himself; the wings of the Agony in the Garden of Gethsemane and the Resurrection are mainly or wholly the work of his assistants.*

Beyond the campsite at the northern end of Detwang, the route crosses over the Tauber and continues along its left bank. This still lies, albeit only just, in Bavaria, as the state boundary with Baden-Württemberg follows the line of the woods to the left, rather than using the obvious demarcation of the river itself. After 3km, there is a paved road to the left offering the opportunity to make a short detour up to Burg Seldeneck, a ruined medieval castle commanding a fine view over the valley. A short distance past this turn-off, the main route crosses the Tauber to pass through Bettwar, which has a church with a half-timbered tower and some impressive large farmsteads. At the far end of the village, the track crosses back to the left bank and ascends gradually, offering a good backwards view.

A further 3km on, there is a junction of three trails at the bridge leading to Tauberscheckenbach. This time the Romantic Road route bypasses the village, and continues along the left bank, where sawmills and other evidence of the logging industry become increasingly prevalent. However, before following this it is again worth making a detour along the other path, which leads uphill to the site of what was once a substantial Celtic settlement. Some sections remain of its defensive wall of stone and wood, which originally stretched for 1.5km. Its history is shrouded in mystery, though it is known to date back to the time of Christ.

Back on the main route, the next logging village to be bypassed is Tauberzell, 2km on from Tauberscheckenbach, which stands at

STAGES 19, 20, 21, 22 & 23

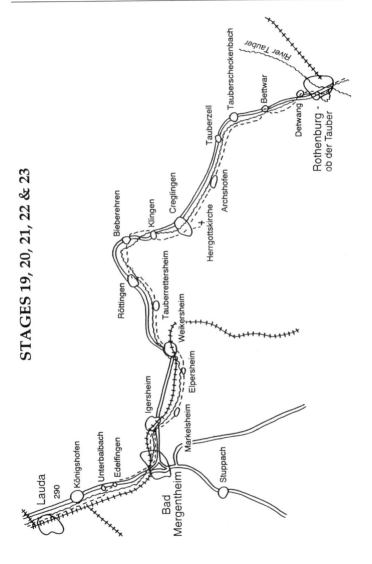

the point where the Tauber starts to assume a north-westerly course. A short distance beyond, the route enters Baden-Württemberg. After a further 2km, it briefly deviates away from the Tauber to go right through the middle of Archshofen, after which it returns once again to the riverside.

Passing opposite Craintal en route, it reaches **CREGLINGEN** after another 3km.

Creglingen

This town was granted civic and market rights in 1349, but has never grown very big, at least in population. Even now, only 5,000 people live in the municipality, which incorporates a dozen outlying villages, including Archshofen and Craintal, spread out over an area of 117sq km.

Creglingen itself has a quaint old-world feel, with many half-timbered houses, some of which are perched directly over fragments of the former ramparts. South of the Stadtkirche (Town Church), which is approached via an impressive flight of steps, is the finest example of half-timbering in town, the **Römschlössle**. This was built in 1589 on an older stone base as a mansion for the prosperous Weinsberg family, and is in the form of a small palace, complete with courtyard and an idiosyncratic octagonal tower. It was recently restored to serve as a conference centre and festive venue.

In an isolated setting 1.5km south of town is the main local attraction, the **Herrgottskirche** (Lord God's Church). The quickest means of access is via the main road, which the Romantic Road cycle route reaches immediately before it crosses into the town centre via the bridge over the Herrgottsbach, the brook named after the church. A far more atmospheric approach, however, is to cross over and follow the path along the side of the Herrgottsbach. This passes through the countryside known, without a trace of irony, as the Herrgottsländle (Lord God's Little Country), a nickname which reflects not only the church's name, but also the local belief that it resembles the Garden of Eden.

The **Herrgottskirche**, which in reality has the dimensions of a chapel rather than a church, was built in Gothic style in the 1380s by the Counts of Hohenlohe-Brauneck, following a ploughman's discovery of a miraculous holy wafer in a nearby field. Externally, the main features are the main northern portal, the curious stair turret on the south side, and the many memorial epitaphs placed on the walls. Inside is an extraordinary set of late Gothic furnishings, including no fewer than four large retables. The polychromed high altar, which illustrates the Passion, is from the circle of the great Nuremberg sculptor Veit Stoss; the Crucifix on the south wall of the nave is even closer to Stoss's style, and may even be by him.

However, the pride and joy of the church is the 11m high limewood altar to the Virgin in the middle of the nave, which was carved by Tilman Riemenschneider around 1510. Set in a filigree shrine specially constructed in order to catch the day's changing light effects, the main scene is not only the artist's masterpiece, but also one of the supreme achievements of the woodcarver's art. Following the adoption of the Reformation in 1530, the altar was closed off and not reopened until 1832 - hence its remarkable state of preservation.

In the mill buildings in the valley immediately below the church is Creglingen's other much touted attraction, the **Fingerhutmuseum** (Thimble Museum), which is billed as the only one of its kind in the world. The subject-matter seems an unlikely one, even when allowance is made for the German penchant for esoteric specialist collections. In fact, it offers a surprisingly entertaining display of thimbles from Roman times to the present day, with an emphasis on items designed as miniature works of art.

For those wishing to explore more of the Creglingen municipal area, the most enticing destination is **FRAUENTAL**, which lies 7km to the north-east of the town in the valley of another Tauber tributary, the Steinach. It can be reached either by road or marked footpath, each of which goes via a different section of the Klosterwald ("Convent Forest").

Dominating the village is the former **Zisterziensinnerinkloster** (Cistercian Convent), which was founded in 1232 under the patronage of the Counts of Hohenlohe-Brauneck, and functioned until 1547, whereupon it served - not inappropriately, given its austere, barn-like appearance - as a granary. Within the Gothic church are no fewer than three separate places of worship: the lower church, or crypt, which is used for Protestant parish worship; the upper church, with its pentagonal apse; and the nuns' gallery, which now contains a museum documenting the convent's history. The key to the church can be picked up, except on Mondays, at house no. 27 in the village.

Some 3km west of Frauental is **Burg Brauneck**, the ancestral seat of the Counts of Hohenlohe-Brauneck, who died out in 1390, soon after the completion of the Herrgottskirche. Substantial parts of their castle still survive in the present complex, which is a working farmstead. Another farm in the vicinity, located in the hamlet of Weidenhof, 2km north-east of Frauental, has gained a place on the tourist circuit for a very different reason. A few years ago the owners, who already offered conventional accommodation to visitors, decided to let spaces in the hay-filled attic as well. Although intended at first as no more than a gimmick, Germany's first Heuhotel ("Hay Hotel") has proved extremely popular.

STAGE 20:
CREGLINGEN TO RÖTTINGEN (12km)
(See map p152/153)

Creglingen was formerly linked with a branch railway to Weikersheim, which hugged the right bank of the Tauber for all but the last 1km of its route, where it switched to the opposite side of the river. Having already been stripped of its rail tracks it was, at the time of writing, in the process of being converted into a cycle path. When this is completed, it may well be chosen as the recommended Romantic Road route, with the official signposts altered accordingly. If not, it will nonetheless provide an alternative to the current designated route described below, which skips from side to side of the Tauber, though mostly lies along the left bank.

From the northern end of Creglingen's main street, Hauptstrasse, the route proceeds along the side of the river, past the bus station and all the way down Kieselalle, where it picks up the cycle- and footpath out of town. After just over 1km, it crosses a small tributary, the Rindbach; almost immediately beyond, it passes out of Baden-Württemberg and re-enters Bavaria, this time the province of Lower Franconia (Unterfranken). Another 1km beyond is Klingen, but the route only skirts this village, bearing right to cross over the bridge and briefly proceed in a southerly direction, before following the track to the left, which continues along the east bank of the Tauber. This crosses the old railway line, then runs through the fields parallel to it for 1.5km, until the path terminates at the road linking Frauental with Bieberehren.

Here it is necessary to turn right along the road for about 50m, then immediately left to continue by the track along the right bank of the Steinach. Having crossed back over the old railway line, the path runs alongside the stream for the short distance to its confluence with the Tauber, which is then followed all the way to the bridge at the southern end of Bieberehren, some 7km from Creglingen. Here the route turns right and follows the main road to the centre of the village, where it turns left, proceeds out of the built-up area and crosses back over the Tauber. For the next 2km the course of the track mirrors the curvaceous course of the river, though it seldom runs very close to the bank. At the Gossenmühle, it crosses over the Tauber yet again, and travels north-westwards towards the main road.

This soon arrives at the little wine-producing town of **RÖTTINGEN**, which nestles between the Tauber and the vineyards on the slopes above.

Röttingen

Even with the absorption of neighbouring villages, including both Klingen and Bieberehren, its population numbers just 1,800. Nonetheless, it has a surprisingly grand air in relation to its tiny size. Most of the **Stadtmauer** (Town Wall) survives, including seven towers which have all been converted into houses. Of these, the most impressive is the **Hundheimer Torturm**, the gateway guarding the western approach road.

Directly opposite is a much remodelled feudal castle, **Burg Brattenstein**, which dates back to the 12th century and was the home of several aristocratic families before becoming the residence of the local administrator of the Würzburg Prince-Bishopric. In summer, its courtyard is the setting for a season of open-air theatre. The central Marktplatz is lined with a number of typical half-timbered houses, and is closed at its western end by the Baroque **Rathaus** (Town Hall). A block to the north is the church of **St Kilian**, which is Romanesque in origin.

Röttingen dubs itself "Stadt der Sonnenuhren" (Town of the Sundials). No fewer than 30 different sundials are scattered throughout the town, and it is their sheer prevalence which is chiefly responsible for endowing it with its distinctive sense of place. They come in all shapes and sizes, range in style from the traditional to the avant-garde, and are of widely varying degrees of sophistication. Some are horizontal in format, others are extremely prominent, while others are easily overlooked, unless armed with the tourist office map showing all the locations. A dozen of the sundials can be seen by following the **Sonnenuhrenweg**, which goes around the perimeter of the Stadtmauer, while four more are in the grounds of Burg Brattenstein.

RÖTTINGEN TO WEIKERSHEIM (8km)
(See map p152/153)

The Romantic Road leaves Röttingen by the Tauber bridge, which is about 200m south of Marktplatz. It continues southwards along Neubronner Strasse, passing one of the 30 sundials, before turning off the road and proceeding to the right along a paved cycle track.

This travels between the river and a predominantly deciduous forest, the Bürgerwald, for the 4km to Tauberrettersheim, where the river is forded by a graceful stone bridge built in 1733 to plans by the great architect Balthasar Neumann. Continuing along the side of the Tauber, the Romantic Road re-enters Baden-Württemberg a further 2km on. After another 1km, it passes directly in front of the little bridge which formerly carried the branch railway over from the right bank of the Tauber. Some 100m ahead, the track meets up with a minor road.

At this junction, it turns sharp left and continues straight ahead through the southern outskirts of **WEIKERSHEIM**, bearing leftwards at the inner ring road, then right into the main shopping street, Hauptstrasse, which leads to the central Marktplatz.

Weikersheim

Grouped around the square are all the main sights of this old courtly town, which currently has a population of just under 8,000. Although none of the family lives there any more, it is the ancestral home of the House of Hohenlohe, which was established by the local lords in the mid-12th century.

The **Stadtkirche** (Town Church) at the eastern end of Marktplatz was founded in 1419 by Conrad von Weinsberg and his wife Anna, a daughter of the Hohenlohe-Weikersheim line. Over the entrance there was formerly a tympanum carved with a depiction of the donors carrying a model of their church, but this has been removed indoors for conservation reasons. Only the hall nave remains of the original building; all the other parts of the fabric date from a large-

Weikersheim, the Schloss, with the Stadtkirche in the background

scale remodelling carried out between 1587 and 1618 in the by then
archaic Gothic style.

On the north side of Marktplatz, the displays of the **Tauberländer**

Dorfmuseum (Tauber Region Village Museum) document the lifestyle and culture of the local farming and vineyard workers. There is a particularly fine collection of traditional costumes, both for everyday wear and for special occasions.

In reality, Weikersheim's Marktplatz was far less a marketplace than a grand forecourt to the **Schloss**. Indeed, the square's present appearance is the result of an 18th century town planning exercise which had this very aim in mind. The arcaded buildings at the western end of the square impart a particular touch of Baroque swagger, reaching out like embracing arms in the manner of the colonnades fronting St Peter's in Rome.

Masonry from the original 12th century fortress survives in the lower parts of the keep, while the north wing preserves part of the medieval moated castle which later emerged. The story of its transformation into the grand palatial residence which can be seen today begins in 1586, when Count Ludwig II decided to re-establish Weikersheim in its long usurped role as the family's main seat. Much of the Renaissance wing is occupied by the sumptuous Rittersaal (Knights' Hall), whose decorations are a hymn of praise to the dynasty and its varied preoccupations.

The **Schlossgarten** (Schloss Garden), which is contemporary with the later parts of the Schloss, is exceptionally well preserved. Bounded by avenues of chestnut trees, it is arranged symmetrically, with formal clipped hedges offset by the blazing colour of the flower arrangements. The decorative sculptures, which are the work of Johann Jakob Sommer and his three sons, are particularly notable. On the balustrade immediately below the Schloss is a series of caricatures of members of the court; these were inspired by the famous engravings of the Lorraine artist Jacques Callot, and are the only intact set of this once popular subject to have survived. In the central pond is a group showing Hercules fighting the Hydra. Like many petty German princes, the Hohenlohes fondly saw analogies between themselves and the mythological hero.

Further evidence of their megalomania can be seen in the unfinished **Orangerie** (Orangery) at the end of the garden, which provides a theatrical backdrop to the Tauber valley beyond. Among the figures represented are those they believed to be their spiritual ancestors - none other than the Emperors of Ancient Assyria, Persia, Greece and Rome.

WEIKERSHEIM TO BAD MERGENTHEIM (13km)
(See map p152/153)

From Weikersheim's Marktplatz, the Romantic Road leads on southwards through the town, crossing both the Vorbach, a tributary stream of the Tauber, and the tracks of the still functioning stretch of the Taubertalbahn (Tauber Valley Railway) which links Weikersheim with Wertheim. The route bears right along the side of the railway, leaving it just before the bridge which carries it back to the northern bank of the Tauber.

It continues via a 2km long track on the south side of the river to Elpersheim. In the centre of the village, it makes a sharp right turn and continues due northwards over the Tauber bridge, and on to the unmanned railway halt a short distance beyond. There it turns sharp left, and proceeds along a pathway between the railway and the river. After 3km, it arrives at the station of Markelsheim, where it crosses back over the Tauber. It proceeds to the centre of this picturesque village, nowadays a part of the municipality of Bad Mergentheim, whose wine-producing tradition dates back at least as far as the 11th century. From the Marktplatz, the way ahead lies to the right, along another track running along the south bank of the Tauber.

After a further 3km the path terminates at the old stone bridge at the entrance to Igersheim, a little town on the opposite bank which has managed to avoid being swallowed up by Bad Mergentheim, despite the fact that there is now very little open countryside separating the two. At this point, the signposts offer a choice of routes to the centre of **BAD MERGENTHEIM**, which is still 3km away.

One possibility is to stick to the southern bank of the Tauber, thus bypassing Igersheim altogether. A short distance beyond the bridge, there is a tunnel under the B19 road, which leads to a cycle track which continues for the remaining distance along the side of the river, with views southwards to a ruined medieval castle, Burg

Neuhaus. The alternative is to cross over the bridge, then immediately turn right, to follow once more the track sandwiched between the railway line and the north bank of the river.

Bad Mergentheim

This is the only spa town along the entire course of the Romantic Road, if the Füssen suburb of Bad Faulenbach, which does not count as part of the official route, is excluded. This is despite the fact that spas (which are readily identifiable by the prefix "Bad") are actually ubiquitous in Germany, as well as in those adjacent parts of Central Europe, such as Bohemia and Silesia, which were formerly under its sway.

The German-speaking world's infatuation with water cures, in which bathing and drinking are of equal importance, dates back many centuries. It is often assumed that they had their heyday in the fin de siècle period of a century ago, when they enjoyed the regular patronage of landed aristocrats from all over Europe. However, although the Bolshevik Revolution and two World Wars decimated this clientèle, the spas in the western part of Germany have enjoyed an unprecedented boom over the last half-century.

Judging from the evidence of excavations, which have led to the uncovering of a Celtic well, the presence of hot saline springs at this point was known to Bronze Age tribes. However they lay forgotten for two millennia, until their rediscovery during a dry spell in 1826 by a shepherd who noticed his flock crowding around a trickle of water close to the north bank of the Tauber. Three years later, the first spa hotel opened.

The northern route from Igersheim enters Bad Mergentheim via the spa quarter, on the opposite side of the railway line from one of the main concentrations of sanatoria and clinics. It passes directly alongside two of the four springs, the Paulusquelle (whose waters are suitable for bathing but not for drinking) and the Albertquelle. As cycling is banned within the boundaries of the **Kuranlage** (Spa Park), it turns left by its entrance and crosses the little bridge over the Tauber to join up with the other route.

The Kuranlage is a beautifully manicured park planted with trees and flowers which is seen at its best in spring and early summer. Notwithstanding the presence of the railway line, which divides it horizontally, it is a wonderful place for quiet strolls. The Karlsquelle, whose waters are the most frequently prescribed of all the local springs, is at its eastern edge, while the Wilhelmsquelle, the first to be discovered, is just south of the railway bridge over the Tauber.

At the heart of the park is the **Wandelhalle** (Pump Room), a glass palace built in 1935 in a style which has echoes of colonial architecture as well as the geometricity characteristic of the Bauhaus movement. In addition to the drinking hall, where the waters can be sampled at elegant marble basins, it has a hall for concerts and dances as well as rooms for a host of other activities. The other main spa buildings, the **Kurhaus** and the **Kurverwaltung** (Spa Reception), are at the northern end of the park. Facing them across Lothar-Daiker-Strasse is the highly prestigious **Klinik Hohenlohe**, a fine example of early 20th century spa architecture.

Just beyond the eastern end of the same street, a short walk north-east from the Karlsquelle, is the **Solymar**, where the spa quarter's ultra-modern public bathing facilities are to be found. Its mineral bath, which is maintained at a constant temperature of 32 degrees, has linked indoor and outdoor sections. There are two other swimming pools: one is equipped with a wave-machine and a 60m long chute, the other is of Olympic-size dimensions. Other facilities include saunas, a solarium, a sun terrace and a games room.

Across the Tauber from the Kuranlage is another park, the Schlosspark, which is named after the vast, rambling complex of the **Deutschordensschloss** (Teutonic Knights' Schloss), the headquarters of Germany's premier chivalrous order from 1525 until its initial suppression by Napoleon in 1806.

The Bläserturm (Trupeter's Tower) above the courtyard still survives from the old medieval castle, which was gradually replaced and expanded throughout virtually the entire duration of the Knights' stay in Mergentheim. The Baroque **Schlosskirche** on the east side of the courtyard is now a Protestant parish church. It was built in 1730-6.

Across the courtyard, an ingenious Renaissance corkscrew staircase from 1574 leads up to the **Schlossmuseum**, which occupies some of the historical chambers of the palace. The most imposing of

Bad Mergentheim, the Wandelhalle

these is the Neoclassical Kapitelsaal (Chapter House), which is nowadays regularly used as a concert hall. Some rooms are used for displays on the history of the order, including valuable treasury items and portraits of all the Mergentheim Grand Masters. There is also documentation on the general history of the town, and a collection of historic dolls' houses.

The bright orange Torbau (Gate Building) with its fancy Renaissance gables connects the Schloss with the compact town centre, which presents a bustling face in total contrast to the serenity of the spa quarter. On the south side of the central Marktplatz is the 16th century **Rathaus** (Town Hall); the arms of the Grand Master who built it are borne by the hero Roland in the fountain in front. The sides of the square are lined with colourful houses erected at various dates by vassals of the order. On the north side are two identical pavilions in a transitional style between Baroque and Neoclassical; one of these contains the tourist office, the other a pharmacy.

Rearing up behind these is the tall tower of the Gothic **Stadtkirche** (Town Church), which was founded by another Crusading order, the Knights of St John. Beside it is the **Spital** (Hospice), with its tiny Rococo chapel. South of Marktplatz is the **Marienkirche** (St Mary's Church), another Gothic building, one that was formerly part of a Dominican monastery. On the north wall of its nave is a magnificent Renaissance funerary monument to Grand Master Walter von Cronburg by the Nuremberg bronze founder Hans Vischer. Opposite is a small prayer chapel whose walls are frescoed with mystical scenes painted by a 14th century friar, Rudolphus von Wimpfen.

For those wishing to explore beyond the town centre, there are two especially worthwhile destinations within the municipal area. The **Wildpark** in the Katzenwald ("Cats' Forest"), 5km south-east along the main road to Crailsheim, is the largest zoo in Europe where animals are kept in conditions which approximate as closely as possible to those of their natural habitats. In all, some 600 different species live in the park, which stretches over 3,000sq m. The best time to visit is in the afternoon, when there are successive feeding sessions of the cormorants, otters, bears, lynxes, birds of prey and wolves. The last of these makes for a spectacular climax: the pack of 30 suddenly emerges from the woods on the approach of the keepers and, hunger sated, disperses equally abruptly a few minutes later. Immediately afterwards, a demonstration of sheepdogs at work takes place. Other attractions include a children's farm and a section of open woodland where visitors are free to walk among the deer.

The village of **STUPPACH**, which lies in the peaceful valley of the same name, some 8km south-east of Bad Mergentheim, would be sunk in total obscurity but for a single fortuitous event. In 1812, its plain Gothic **Pfarrkirche** (Parish Church) found itself the inheritor of a painting of the Madonna and Child that had formerly belonged to the Teutonic Knights. At the time, it was implausibly attributed to Rubens, but it is now known to have been painted in 1519 by one of Germany's rarest and most admired (as well as most mysterious) artists, Mathis Gothardt-Neithardt, otherwise known as Grünewald. The scene is painted with all the visionary intensity characteristic of this master, yet also has passages of great lyrical beauty, such as the exquisite still life in the foreground. Stuppach can be reached via the B19 road, or by a marked footpath running from Neunkirchen, at the southernmost end of the built-up part of Bad Mergentheim.

BAD MERGENTHEIM TO LAUDA (12km)
(See map p152/153)

The key landmark for the route out of Bad Mergentheim is the Wolfgangsbrücke (St Wolfgang's Bridge) over the Tauber, which takes its name from the Gothic Wolfgangskapelle (St Wolfgang's Chapel) at its northern end. It lies about 500m west of the Klinik Hohenlohe, separated from it by the length of Theodor-Klotzbücher-Strasse. From Markptplatz, the distance is twice as long, the easiest approach being north along Kirchstrasse to Gänsmarkt, then right into Härterichstrasse, over the railway level crossing and then along Wolfgangstrasse.

Once over the bridge, there is a sharp left turn into Edelfinger Strasse. A short distance beyond, the track loops down to travel along the side of the Tauber, before rejoining the street at the end of the built-up area. Soon after, it meets up with the main northbound road through the Tauber valley, on the right-hand side of which is a special track for cyclists and walkers. This is followed as far as Edelfingen, which is still part of the Bad Mergentheim municipality.

Towards the end of the village, the route crosses over the main road and continues downhill, before making a right turn to travel through market gardens and orchards towards Unterbalbach, which is part of the next municipality, Lauda-Königshofen. Unterbalbach itself, which once had a substantial Jewish population, is dominated by the Pfarrkirche St Markus (Parish Church of St Mark) of 1824, which is basically Neoclassical in style, albeit with a few anachronistic Baroque touches. The route follows a somewhat zigzag course around the outskirts of the village, before crossing over the Tauber by the little bridge to the west.

It then proceeds northwards along the path which runs between the railway line and the river, initially with woodland to the right. After 2km, it arrives at the B292 road. At this point, there is the option of making a detour eastwards over the bridge to **KÖNIGSHOFEN**, the smaller of the two main parts of the double town. *Its main claim to fame is the Königshofer Messe (Königshofen Fair), a sort of small-scale version of Munich's celebrated Oktoberfest, which is held over a ten-day period each September. However, the town itself is pleasant enough, retaining fragments of its medieval walls as well as some impressive half-timbered mansions. The Pfarrkirche St Mauritius (Parish Church of St Maurice) is a Neoclassical building of 1836, but its tower is Romanesque by origin, with a Gothic upper storey and a Baroque helmet.*

The marked Romantic Road route bypasses Königshofen, turning left along the B292, then almost immediately right to pick up another path travelling between the railway and the river. From Königshofen station, it continues on for 2km to **LAUDA**, the most recent addition to the list of official staging-posts on the Romantic Road. Notwithstanding this honour, the sights of the town can comfortably be covered in an hour or two. Its main merit is that it is a very convenient touring base, being a rail junction with direct services to Würzburg, as well as up and down the Tauber valley.

Lauda

The route enters Lauda along Tauberstrasse, and it is worth continuing to the end of the street to see the three-arched **Tauberbrücke** (Tauber Bridge). It was first built in 1512; the carved Crucifix was added in 1593, the shrine in 1644, and the statue of St Johann Nepomuk in 1732. Doubling back a little way, a tunnel leads under the elevated rail track to Bahnhofstrasse. Just to the left is the **Liebfrauenkirche** (Church of Our Lady), a cemetery chapel built in late Renaissance style by order of Prince-Bishop Julius von Echter, who commissioned many of Würzburg's finest buildings.

The best approach to the town centre is via Spitalgasse, two blocks west of Bahnhofstrasse, which takes its name from the timber-framed former **Spital** (Hospital). This alley terminates at the main street, Rathausstrasse, where there are several more examples of half-timbering. Among them is the Weinbauerhaus (Vintner's House), which is now home to the **Heimatmuseum** (Local Museum). This has displays on wine production, handicrafts and the tradition annual Fasnacht (Carnival) celebrations, but is unfortunately open on Sundays only. At the top end of the street is the **Oberes Tor** (Upper Gate) of 1496, a rare surviving part of the medieval town walls.

From midway along Rathausstrasse, Pfarrstrasse leads north to the **Stadtkirche St Jakobus der Ältere** (Parish Church of St James the Elder), a typical example of Franconian Baroque. Alongside is the mid-14th century **Pulverturm** (Powder Tower), the only other extant part of the municipal defences.

LAUDA TO TAUBERBISCHOFSHEIM (8km)

The way out of Lauda lies along the northern stretch of Kirchstrasse. Initially, the route runs along the left-hand side of the railway line. After about 1km, the latter splits into two forks, with one continuing down the Tauber valley, the other branching off over the river on its journey towards Würzburg. Almost immediately afterwards, the Romantic Road crosses the tunnel under the former, at which point there is a view across the river to Gerlachsheim. *This village is the most picturesque in the Lauda-Königshofen municipality, with two notable sights in the stone bridge over the Grünbach, a Tauber tributary, and the Baroque church of a former Premonstratensian monastery. It is well worth making a detour to see it, though it is necessary to do this via the Tauberbrücke in Lauda, as the bridge ahead carries the Würzburg railway only.*

The Romantic Road meanwhile swings round to assume a northerly course, travelling through the fields between the Tauber railway and the river. After a further 2km, it arrives at the orchards on the outskirts of **DISTELHAUSEN**, passing directly in front of the Gothic **Wolfgangskapelle** (St Wolfgang's Chapel). At this point, there is the possibility of a quick detour into the village itself, which is part of the Tauberbischofsheim municipality. *It is best known for its brewery, whose wide range of beers, some of which have won national awards, are available on tap in most of the region's inns. The **Pfarrkirche** (Parish Church), built from 1731-8, is a typical example of Franconian Baroque, with a single tower, a flat ceilinged interior, and an integrated set of furnishings. It has been attributed to Balthasar Neumann, though it is unlikely that the great architect was involved in more than a consultative capacity.*

From the Wolfgangskapelle, the route continues northwards; from this point onward woods, rather than fields, lie to the west. It goes under the massive viaduct of the A81/E41 motorway, and continues on to **BITTIGHEIM**, a little over 1km beyond Distelhausen, and passes right through the middle of the village.

*The **Pfarrkirche** (Parish Church), which is a decade younger than Distelhausen's, is very similar in style and has likewise been associated with the name of Balthasar Neumann. A number of wayside shrines are dotted around Bittigheim, and one of the most attractive can be seen at the exit to the village.*

It is then little more than 1km to **TAUBERBISCHOFSHEIM** itself. On approaching the town, the path swings slightly westwards, crossing under the B27 and over a Tauber tributary, the Brehmbach, before reaching the line of the fortifications which formerly encircled the town. Here it bears right towards the Tauber, continuing for a short distance along the side of the river, past the war memorial and

STAGES 24 & 25

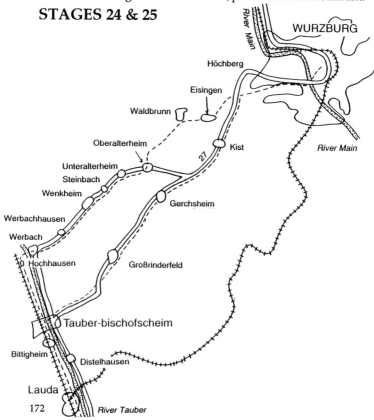

on towards the road bridge, which serves as the reference point for the two alternative routes out of town.

Tauberbischofsheim

Until the mid-19th century, the town was known simply as Bischofsheim, which means "Bishop's Home". This refers to its long role as a secondary residence of the Archbishop-Electors of the Rhenish city of Mainz, who were among the most powerful grandees in medieval Germany, also holding the title of Archchancellor of the Holy Roman Empire.

The town grew up around a convent, the first in Germany, which was founded around 735 by the English-born missionary St Boniface, who later made Mainz the main centre of the Church north of the Alps. In 1237, it was officially confirmed as the eastern frontier-post of the territories of the archbishopric, retaining this role until the secularization of 1803. After a brief period under the Princes of Leiningen, it became part of the new Grand Duchy of Baden. Nowadays, not content with being a mere country town, it promotes itself as the world fencing metropolis. Since 1976, its fencing academy has enjoyed national status, and has been the training ground for the German teams which have dominated several Olympiads.

The main street, Hauptstrasse, runs horizontally all the way through the historic part of town. The most notable buildings on the eastern section of the street are the half-timbered **Lieberhaus** of 1628 and the **Haus Mackert**, a sumptuous Baroque town palace built in 1744 for a wine merchant. Just beyond the latter is the church of **St Lioba**, likewise Baroque and formerly part of a Franciscan monastery. It is named after the town's first abbess, who was a relation (possibly even a sister) of St Boniface.

The church closes off the southern side of Martkplatz, at the opposite end of which is the **Rathaus** (Town Hall), a Neo-Gothic building of 1865. At the north-eastern corner of the square is the half-timbered **Alte Post** (Old Post Office), built in 1602 by the Thurn und Taxis dynasty, which held the German postal monopoly for some 250 years, thus establishing the basis for the family fortune which is still reckoned to be the largest in the country. Further along the northern side of Marktplatz is the **Sternapotheke** ("Star

Pharmacy"). This splendid example of timber-framed architecture, with its humorous friezes of carved heads, is a faithful reconstruction made from drawings of the destroyed original.

Continuing up Hauptstrasse, an alley leads right to the **Sebastianuskapelle** (St Sebastian's Chapel), which was built in 1476 in late Gothic style. There are actually two chapels, one on top of the other. The lower, entered via a portal whose tympanum has a carving of the Last Judgment, is now a war memorial; the upper, reached by the outside stairway, is still used for services. Opposite is the imposingly large **Stadtkirche St Martin** (Town Church of St Martin). At first glance, this appears to be a Gothic church with a Baroque spire, but in fact the whole building is a pastiche, built in 1910-14.

South of Hauptstrasse is the town's other dominant building, the **Schloss** of the Mainz archbishops. Substantial parts remain of the 13th century fortress, including the 28m high Türmersturm (Watchman's Tower), which has become the symbol of the town. In the second half of the 15th century, various additions were made, including the oriel window and the step-gabled east wing, while the timber-framed building beside the tower was not erected until the early 17th century.

The oddly titled **Tauberfränkisches Landschaftsmuseum** (Tauber-Franconian Landscape Museum) now occupies part of the Schloss, including the two main halls of the 13th century castle, whose ceilings are supported by huge oak pillars. Of these, the entrance hall contains weapons, boundary stones delineating the borders of the Mainz archbishopric, and a magnificent early 9th century capital from the great basilica in Fulda which formerly stood on the site of St Boniface's martyrdom. The hall above has displays of sacred art; elsewhere the exhibits range from archaeological finds to colourful traditional costumes and furniture in styles from Renaissance to Biedermeier.

TAUBERBISCHOFSHEIM TO WÜRZBURG (39km)
(See map p172)

Any major touring route needs to have an appropriate climax and Würzburg, one of Germany's most attractive and rewarding cities, makes for a fitting terminus to the Romantic Road. The journey from Tauberbischofsheim is one of the longest stages of the entire route: it is lacking in notable historic sights, but as compensation offers a good deal of pleasantly unspoiled scenery. Walkers certainly need to allocate a full day to cover this stage, which (because of the absence of obvious diversions) is easier to pace than any other.

There are two possible routes, which only converge towards the end. The first of these is very direct, and at 32km is a full 7km shorter than the other. Although this might be considered a considerable advantage, it is the only real point in its favour, a major drawback being the virtual absence of any special tracks for cyclists and walkers.

From the eastern end of Tauberbishofsheim's Hauptstrasse, this route crosses over the river to the suburb on the opposite bank, which bears the very logical name of Über der Tauberbrücke ("Over the Tauber Bridge"). From there it bears left and follows Albert-Schweizer-Strasse to the end of the built-up area, proceeding along a minor road which cuts through the rather grandly titled Grosser Forst ("Great Forest"). It emerges from this to join the B27 at the southern end of the village of Grossrinderfeld, 8km from Tauberbischofsheim. The road is then followed for the remaining 25km to Würzburg.

The newer alternative route, which has the advantage of a good deal of specially laid track, is far preferable. It likewise begins at the eastern end of Tauberbischofsheim's Hauptstrasse, but does not cross the river, instead following the Liebliches Taubertal route signs round the inner ring road, before turning right into Pestalozzistrasse, which leads northwards out of town. A track runs alongside the road, though some way back from the river, for the 5km to Hochhausen.

Just beyond the northern edge of the village, the Romantic Road parts company with the Tauber valley route, turning right to cross the bridge. On the other side, a short distance uphill, is the larger village of Werbach. With a couple of inns and a guesthouse, it is the last place before Würzburg with much in the way of accommodation, and for walkers, in particular, is worth considering as an overnight stop in preference to Tauberbischofsheim.

The route itself skirts the southern edge of Werbach, leaving the road at the end of the built-up area, and continuing along a path which runs alongside the Welzbach, a Tauber tributary. After 2km this passes the Neo-Gothic Wallfahrtskirche (Pilgrimage Church), romantically set below the wooded Höhberg (321m). The miracle-working spring which gave rise to the pilgrimage is reached by means of a covered passageway which is located directly behind the church's high altar, though it is accessible only from the outside of the building.

A short distance onwards, the route crosses to the right bank of the Welzbach. Skirting the edge of Werbachhausen, it continues onwards along the side of the woods above the river, passing several mills in the course of the 3km to Wenkheim. Here it crosses back to the left side of the stream and runs parallel to the road. Soon after, it leaves Baden-Württemberg and re-enters the Bavarian province of Lower Franconia.

At Steinbach, 2km on, it crosses back to the right side of the Welzbach once again and follows the stream to Unteralterheim, which is located at the head of the valley. Here the route joins up with the road again, following it as far as Oberalterheim, just over 1km beyond. In the middle of this village, the Romantic Road sign points uphill to the left. When the road forks, the temptation is to bear right, but this track, which goes in the desired north-easterly direction, terminates abruptly in the middle of a field. Instead, it is necessary to continue on uphill via the left-hand fork, which then descends through the fields to the Irtenberger Wald, an extensive mixed forest. It is criss-crossed by trails, but the lack of waymarking unfortunately means that further exploration is inadvisable, as it is all too easy to get lost. The only signposted path is that followed by the Romantic Road itself, which cuts through the narrowest part of the forest, emerging to descend to one of the tunnels under the A3/E41 motorway.

Once over, it ascends towards Waldbrunn. As it approaches the outskirts, the track turns sharp right and travels north-eastwards along the edge of the village until reaching a road, which goes 2km east to Eisingen. It passes right the way through this long elongated village, then turns left down a farm track, which travels north for a further 2km before turning right towards Höchberg, one of the string of satellite towns around Würzburg. This eventually leads straight ahead to the main street, Hauptstrasse, which forms part of the B27 from Tauberbischofsheim.

As the road descends, there is a thrilling view of Würzburg, with the hilltop Marienberg fortress in the foreground, and tantalizing glimpses of the city centre skyline beyond. The signposted route of the Romantic Road follows Leistenstrasse all the way down the southern side of the Marienberg and the Kuhbach ("Cow Stream"), turning left at the foot of the hill to proceed northwards along the waterfront of the River Main, crossing over the Friedensbrücke and continuing eastwards to the Hauptbahnhof or main railway station, the official finishing-point. It is, however, slightly quicker to descend to the Friedensbrücke along the northern side of the Marienberg, via Höchberger Strasse, Wörthstrasse and Luitpoldstrasse.

Würzburg

WÜRZBURG, the capital of the Bavarian province of Lower Franconia, is a city blessed with a multitude of riches. It has a wonderful natural setting, spreading out over both the hilly left bank and the low-lying right bank of the River Main; it is an internationally renowned centre for wine production, with the vineyards themselves occupying surprisingly prominent positions within the townscape; and it boasts a varied legacy of artistic and architectural masterpieces of the very highest quality.

Celts are known to have inhabited the site as far back as 1000BC, though a continuous history of settlement does not begin until the Dark Ages. In 689, the Irish bishop St Kilian was martyred there, together with his assistants St Kolonat and St Totnan, while on a mission to convert the local Franks. However, Christianity soon

Würzburg, the Scherenbergtor and the Kiliansturm in the Festung Marienberg

established a firm hold in the area, and in 742 St Boniface made Würzburg the seat of a bishop, appointing his fellow-Englishman St Burghard (Burkard in German) as the first holder of the see.

The city was first fortified around the year 1000, and gained market rights in 1030. In 1156, it hosted the wedding of Emperor Friedrich Barbarossa to Beatrix of Burgundy, and from 1168 the title of Duke of Franconia was thenceforth conferred on the ruling Prince-Bishop. Medieval Germany's greatest lyric poet, Walther von der Vogelweide, was granted a fief in Würzburg by Barbarossa's grandson, Emperor Friedrich II, and lived in the city until his death in 1230. The next major figure in Würzburg's cultural pantheon was the sculptor Tilman Riemenschneider, who settled there in 1483, executing a stream of hauntingly evocative and instantly recognizable carvings which adorn churches throughout Franconia. His contemporary, the painter Mathis Grünewald, is believed to have been a native of the city, though no works by him can be seen there.

Julius Echter von Mespelbrunn, who refounded the university in 1582 and initiated an extensive building programme, is the most celebrated of Würzburg's Prince-Bishops. However, the most fruitful period of architectural patronage came in the 18th century. Successive members of the Schönborn family, a dynasty which specialized in the acquisition of major ecclesiastical offices throughout Germany, recognized the unique genius of Balthasar Neumann, who arrived in the city as a humble metalworker yet developed into the most brilliantly innovative and accomplished architect of 18th century Europe.

With the secularization of the Prince-Bishopric in 1802, Würzburg was incorporated into Bavaria and ceased to be a major artistic centre. However, the 19th century saw the university gain an ever growing scientific reputation, its prestige reaching a climax in 1895, with Wilhelm Conrad Röntgen's discovery of X-rays. At the very end of World War II, much of Würzburg was flattened in an air raid: indeed, it sustained more damage than any German city other than Dresden. Reconstruction work continued over several decades, with the result that most of the damage is now little more than a bad memory.

Würzburg's most prominent monument is the **Festung**

Marienberg (Marienberg Fortress) which overlooks the city centre from its lofty hilltop position above neat terraced vineyards on the left side of the Main. This huge complex, begun in 1201, served as the main residence of the Prince-Bishops from 1253 until 1719. During this time, it gradually evolved from a medieval castle into a Renaissance palace, which in turn was given a strongly fortified character during the Baroque period by the addition of a ring of bastions.

The most convenient means of access is via the steep footpath which leads up from Zeller Strasse on the north side. Entry is via the main outer gateway, the Neutor (New Gate) of 1650, which is carved with the armorial bearings of the Schönborn dynasty. From there, the path continues uphill and passes through three more gates in the bastions before entering the first courtyard. On the east side of this is the Echterbastei (Echter Bastion) of 1605; on the north and west and south sides, the Zeughaus (Arsenal), which was built by Balthasar Neumann's teacher, the military engineer Andreas Müller, from 1702-12.

These buildings now house the **Mainfränkisches Museum** (Main-Franconian Museum), which is best known for having the world's largest and most important collection of sculptures by Tilman Riemenschneider. Among the works on display are the originals of most of the sandstone statues he made for the Marienkapelle in the town centre, including the sublimely beautiful figures of Adam and Eve. Numerous limewood carvings by the same sculptor, including an exquisite little Madonna and Child and a pair of candelabra-bearing angels, are also on view. Other exhibits of special note include sketches by members of the Tiepolo family; the originals of the Rococo garden sculptures from the Prince-bishops' summer residence at Veitshochheim a short distance down the Main; and a collection of old wooden wine presses.

A gateway adorned with a statue of St Michael conquering the dragon leads through the Echterbastei to the second courtyard. At the far end is the original moat, which is protected by a circuit of medieval walls with round towers. Guarding the entrance to the third and innermost courtyard is a late 15th century bailey, named the Scherenbergtor (Scherenberg Gate) in honour of the Prince-bishop who commissioned it. Statues of the three martyred Irish saints are placed immediately over the archway. Rearing up behind is the Kiliansturm (St Kilian's Tower), which gained its present Renaissance shape in 1607.

The freestanding tower in the middle of the inner courtyard is the Bergfried (Keep), the very first part of the castle to be built. Ironically, it is not the oldest building within the complex, that honour belonging to the **Marienkirche** (St Mary's Church) or Rundkirche (Round Church), the original cathedral of the Würzburg diocese, which stands behind. This dates back to the 8th century, and has a reasonable claim to be regarded as the oldest intact church in Germany, though it has been remodelled on several occasions. Memorial effigies of several Prince-bishops are embedded in the pavement, while the cupola is decorated with late Renaissance stuccowork.

Alongside is the octagonal **Brunnenhaus** (Well House), an elegant Renaissance pavilion adorned with reliefs of the Old Testament figures of Daniel, Samson and Jeremiah and topped with a statue of the goddess Fortuna. The well itself, which is 103m deep, is much older, having been dug through the rock in the early 14th century to ensure a constant supply of fresh water to the fortress.

The eastern courtyard wing, known as the **Fürstenbau** (Princes' Building), was the residence of the Prince-bishops. It incorporates some medieval features, including the Randersacker Turm (Randersacker Tower) at the south-east corner, but was progressively remodelled to suit changing tastes. War and neglect have left little in the way of original interior decoration and furnishings, but the apartments have been put to good use to house displays on the history of the city. The star exhibit is the oldest surviving battle standard in Germany, the St Kilian's Banner of 1266. Also on view are objects found in archaeological excavations of the Würzburg area; the treasury of the Prince-bishops; and models showing the city as it was in the 16th century and after the 1945 bombings.

On the terrace immediately below the palace is the **Fürstengarten** (Princes' Garden), which is laid out in the formal style of the Italian Baroque, with pavilions at either end. It is seen at its most glorious when the roses are in full bloom in the early summer, but it is always worth a visit for the sake of what is arguably the best of all the wonderful panoramic views the city has to offer.

Back down on Zeller Strasse, the **Deutschhauskirche**, which was built in the 13th century by the Teutonic Knights, can be seen immediately to the north. Its tower is late Romanesque in style, but the main body of the building is early Gothic. A curiosity is the passageway under the tribune gallery, which provides a link between Zeller Strasse and Schottenganger, a large square where public executions were formerly held. The royal palace where the wedding of Frederick Barbarossa took place formerly stood alongside the church.

At the far end of Schottenganger is the **Dom-Bosco-Kirche**, the monastic church of a congregation of Salesian Fathers. This incorporates the towers and chancel of the former Jakobskirche (St James' Church), which was founded by Irish monks in the 12th century and occupied by a Scottish Benedictine congregation from 1595 until the Napoleonic secularization. Tragically, the church was damaged beyond meaningful restoration by British bombs in 1945, and had to be given a completely new nave.

Overlooking the waterfront directly below the Marienberg is **St Burkard**, a medieval church which has survived in much better shape. Its Romanesque nave dates back to the first half of the 11th century, whereas the late Gothic transept and choir were not added until the end of the 15th century, and again have a covered passageway allowing the street to pass underneath. Among the furnishings are a medieval collection box in the shape of a capital and a tender carving by Riemenschneider of the Madonna and Child which was later given a covering of polychromy.

The Nikolausberg, the hill immediately south of the Marienberg, is crowned by the **Käppele**, a twin-towered pilgrimage church built by Balthasar Neumann in 1748-52. It is approached via a double stairway with terraces, which are lined by fourteen pavilions containing life-sized sculptural depictions of the Stations of the Cross by the court sculptor Peter Wagner. From the top, there are marvellous views across to the Marienberg and down to the city centre. The church was decorated by the Wessobrunn stuccoist Johann Michael Feichtmayr, and frescoed by the Augsburg artist Matthäus Günther, who depicted the Glorification of the Virgin Mary on the main cupola, and the story of the foundation of the pilgrimage in the sanctuary.

By far the most picturesque of the bridges linking the two parts of the city centre is the middle one of the trio, the pedestrian-only **Alte Mainbrücke** (Old Main Bridge). It was begun in 1473 on the site of an older bridge, though it was not until 1603 that the wooden arches were replaced by sturdier stone constructions. The twelve over-life-size statues of saints were added during the 18th century.

To the north along the right-hand quayside is the ingenious structure known as the **Alter Kranen** (Old Cranes). Built around 1770 by Franz Ignaz Neumann (son of Balthasar) it incorporates two separate winding mechanisms, which allowed ships to be loaded and unloaded simultaneously. The jetty alongside is the departure-point for the summertime pleasure cruises up and down the Main; destinations include the aforementioned palace at Veitshochheim and the fortified towns of Ochsenfurt and Sulzfeld.

Eastwards along the broad Juliuspromenade is the **Juliusspital**, an institution for the poor and sick named in honour of its founder, Julius Echter. The original Renaissance buildings burned down in 1699, to be replaced by the present palatial complex, which was designed by Antonio Petrini, the Italan architect who introduced the Baroque style to the city. Within the Fürstenbau (Princes' Building) on the northern side of the courtyard is a Rococo pharmacy, a completely intact period gem. In the peaceful gardens to the rear is a fountain made in 1706 by Jakob van der Auvera which bears allegorical figures representing the four main rivers of Franconia. The Juliusspital's charitable activities have always been funded from its 170 hectares of vineyards, which produce some of Franconia's finest wines. These can be sampled in the excellent yet moderately priced restaurant which forms part of the complex.

Immediately to the south, at the top end of Schönbornstrasse, is the **Augustinerkirche** (St Augustine's Church), which was formerly part of a Dominican monastery founded by St Albertus Magnus. Only the choir remains from the original Gothic building; the nave and facade were added by Balthasar Neumann in 1741. Sadly, only a small part of the luxuriant stuccowork of the interior survived the last war.

A little further east, reached via Hauger Pfarrgasse, is **Stift Haug**, which was built by Petrini between 1670 and 1691. It has a richly decorated twin-towered facade and a large central dome, but lost most of its interior decoration in 1945. At the high altar is a monumental painting of the Crucifixion, which was painted in the workshop of Tintoretto in 1583.

On Theaterstrasse to the south is the **Bürgerspital**, the older of Würzburg's two great charitable institutions, founded by a wealthy burgher in 1319. The original Gothic church still survives, though its most valuable art treasures have been moved to the Mainfränkisches Museum; the rest of the complex was rebuilt in the early 18th century in Baroque style by Andreas Müller. Most of the Bürgerspital's income comes from its 140 hectares of vineyards, which produce particularly fine dry wines, and it has a restaurant which is a worthy rival to that of the Juliusspital. In accordance with the wishes of the founders, the residents are supplied with a quarter-litre of wine each weekday, and a half-litre on Sundays.

Eichhornstrasse leads west from Theaterstrasse back to Schönbornstrasse, from where it is only a few paces to the Markt. At the corner of the square is the most ornate mansion in the city, the **Haus zum Falken** ("House to the Falcon"), which is now home to one of the tourist offices. The magnificent Rococo stuccowork of the facade, in which falcons are prominent, dates from 1751.

Alongside is the Gothic **Marienkapelle** (St Mary's Chapel) which, in spite of its name, is a full-sized hall church. It was begun in 1377 on the site of a Jewish ritual bath house. The main body of the building was completed in 1441, though the tower was not raised until 1479, while the openwork spire was only added in 1857-8. There are three richly sculptured portals.

Just off the south-east corner of the Markt is the **Grafeneckart** or **Rathaus** (Town Hall). It was originally built in the 13th century as the seat of the episcopal administrator, and from this period comes the Wenzelsaal (Wenzel Hall), a splendid room in the Transitional style between Romanesque and Gothic named after King Wenzel the Lazy who promised but failed to grant Würzburg the status of a Free Imperial City. In 1316 the building assumed its present function and has been expanded on several occasions: the western extension, the Roter Bau (Red Building), was added in late Renaissance style in 1659.

Domstrasse leads east from the Rathaus to the **Dom** (Cathedral), which bears a dedication to the three Irish martyrs. One of Germany's

Würzburg, the west portal of the Marienkapelle

185

largest Romanesque churches, it was constructed between 1135 and 1188, though the slender east towers were not completed until 1237.

Although the exterior of the Dom was fully restored following severe war damage, the reconstruction of the interior is an intentional compromise between the old and the new - hence the austere flat ceiling of the nave, and the avant-garde high altar, which presents a vision of the New Jerusalem.

Alongside the Dom, occupying the presumed site of the martyrdom of St Kilian and his companions, is the **Neumünster** ("New Minster"). In the crypt, a modern shrine contains the mortal remains of St Kilian. Riemenschneider made imaginary portrait busts of the saints to adorn the church's high altar. Those that can be seen today are copies of the originals, which were destroyed in 1945, but the stone statue of the Madonna and Child under the dome is a genuine work by the same master.

On the north side of the Neumünster is the **Lusamgärtchen**, a little garden laid out around the roofless surviving wing of the 12th century cloister. It contains the grave of Walter von der Vogelweide, which is flanked, in accordance with the minstrel's own wishes, with flat basins filled with water for birds to drink. Immediately to the east are several fine old mansions. These include the Renaissance **Hof Conti**, with its fine oriel window. Nowadays it serves as the residence of the local bishop.

Just south of the Dom on Plattnerstrasse is another notable mansion, the **Marmelsteiner Hof**, which was built by Balthasar Neumann in 1747. It now houses the diocesan exhibition gallery, which mounts regular changing exhibitions. Continuing southwards along Schontalstrasse, the **Franziskanerkirche** (Franciscan Church) can be seen to the right. Founded in 1249, it is built in the plain Gothic style favoured by the mendicant orders, and houses a Pietà by Riemenschneider.

A little further south, the northern side of Neubaustrasse is dominated by the huge Renaissance facade of the **Alte Universität** (Old University), which was begun in 1582 to plans by Georg Robin, who later built the Schloss at Weikersheim. In 1696 Antonio Petrini added a splendid Baroque tower to the **Neubaukirche** at the western end of the complex. This is no longer used for worship, serving instead as a concert hall.

Würzburg, the Residenz seen from the Hofgarten

It is then just a short walk to the **Residenz**, the former palace of the Prince-bishops. There could be no more fitting way to end - or begin - a journey along the Romantic Road than with a visit to this great building, which shares with the Wieskirche the honour of being included on UNESCO's World Heritage List.

A true product of the Age of Absolutism, the Residenz was begun in 1720 under the patronage of Prince-bishop Johann Philipp Franz von Schönborn, in the wake of his decision to transfer the seat of the court from the Marienberg back to the city centre. Right from the start, it was intended that the new residential palace would rival that of any of the royal houses of Europe. To this end, Lukas von Hildebrandt, an architect at the Imperial court in Vienna, and Maximilian von Welsch, who held the same position in the Archbishopric of Mainz, were hired to work on the project, and further advice was sought from the French king's architects, Robert de Cotte and German Boffrand. However, construction was left largely in the hands of Balthasar Neumann, who was, for the most part, successful in imposing his own ideas. By 1744, the exterior of the building was finished, though work on the interior went on until

1781, nearly three decades after Neumann's death.

The Residenz has a U-shaped groundplan, with a cour d'honneur and four inner courtyards. Thanks to the allegorical sculptural decoration by Johann van der Auvera, the elevations of the former are strongly festive in character. In contrast, the north and south wings, whose central pavilions are oval in shape, are relatively austere in appearance. However, a lighter touch is evident in the main garden front, which is strongly Viennese in spirit.

Impressive as the exterior is, it is rather overshadowed by the magnificence of the interior. This begins in a deliberately understated way with the low-ceilinged entrance hall, off which is the graceful Gartensaal (Garden Hall).

The darkness of the vestibule only serves to accentuate the magnificence of the famed Treppenhaus (Staircase), which leads up to an airily light gallery. Purely from a technical point of view, it is an astonishing tour-de-force, being covered by a single unsupported stone vault of some 600 sq m. In response to the taunts of Hildebrandt, who claimed it was bound to collapse, Neumann offered to have a battery of artillery fired off it. This experiment was never carried out, but full vindication of his design came in 1945, when it held firm against the aerial bombardment.

In 1752-3, a decade after its construction, the vault was covered with what still ranks as the largest fresco in the world. This was painted by one of the greatest decorative artists of all time, the Venetian Giovanni Battista Tiepolo, who was aided by his sons Giovanni Domenico and Lorenzo. An allegory extolling the Würzburg Prince-bishopric in the most immodest way imaginable, it shows the four continents then known paying respect to the holder of the see, Carl Philipp von Greifenklau, who is transported in triumph to Heaven in the centre of the composition.

At the top of the staircase is the Weisser Saal (White Hall), whose walls are covered with white and grey stuccowork on military themes by Antonio sBossi. The Kaisersaal (Imperial Hall) beyond is the centrepiece of the palace, and the room reserved for the Emperor on his visits to the city. Here Bossi's gilded stuccowork provides a glittering framework for Tiepolo's frescoes, which glorify the concept of the Holy Roman Empire and Würzburg's part within it.

To the right is a suite of state rooms, among which is the

Spiegelkabinett (Mirror Cabinet), a unique work of its kind. Such rooms are standard features of German palaces, but normally feature porcelain displayed in front of recessed mirrors set in wood panelling. Here, however, the walls consist entirely of glass panels decorated on the back with exotic pictures. Completely destroyed in 1945, the Spiegelkabinett was painstakingly recreated from old drawings in a project that was only completed in 1987.

Another suite of rooms to the left of the Kaisersaal culminates in the Grünes Lackzimmer (Green Lacquer Room), a gorgeous example of the very last phase of Würzburg Rococo. This leads directly to the north wing, where a collection of Baroque and Rococo paintings, including several works by the Tiepolos, is hung. The dignified Ingelheimer Zimmern (Ingelheim Rooms) beyond were the last to be completed, and are already Neoclassical in style.

In order not to spoil the overall symmetry, the **Hofkirche** (Court Church) was incorporated into the south-west pavilion of the Residenz. It is a brilliant early example of the spatial illusionism that was to become one of Neumann's trademarks: the interior, based on a series of ovals, appears to be much larger than it actually is. The colourful decoration was designed by Hildebrandt, while the two side altars, showing the Fall of the Rebel Angels and the Assumption, are both by Giovanni Battista Tiepolo.

From the courtyard alongside, a staircase leads up to the University's **Martin-von-Wagner-Museum**. This is in two parts, which are opened alternately. In the mornings and on every other Saturday, the gallery of paintings and sculptures, which includes works by Riemenschneider and Tiepolo, can be seen. At other times, the collection of Classical antiquities is on view.

The **Hofgarten** (Court Garden), which is entered via beautiful wrought-iron grilles, is a worthy backdrop to the Residenz. Because of the proximity of the eastern stretch of the municipal defences, the site was very restricted in size. It had therefore to be laid out as a series of small gardens, with terraces added to create extra space, and these intersect with one another to form a satisfying whole. Johann Peter Wagner carved the charming garden sculptures, which include mythological scenes, portraits of children, vases and cartouches.

APPENDIXES

1: Opening Times

The following are the current opening hours for the museums and monuments described in the text, listed in the order in which they appear. Inevitably, these times are subject to change, but alterations are unlikely to be drastic. Most of the attractions listed charge for admission, though some are free.

The only churches included on this list are those which enforce rigid entry times and/or have a mandatory entrance fee. Almost all the other major churches described in the text are open daily from early morning until early evening. In some cases, however, the grille which gives access to the main body of the building is locked for up to two hours in the middle of the day.

Füssen
Bayerische Staatsgalerie
April to October Tuesday to Sunday 11am to 4pm; November to March Tuesday to Sunday 2pm to 4pm.

Museum der Stadt Füssen
April to October Tuesday to Sunday 11am to 4pm; November to March Tuesday to Sunday 2pm to 4pm.

Hohenschwangau
Schloss Hohenschwangau
Guided tours daily April to September 9am to 5.30pm; October to March 10am to 4pm.

Schloss Neuschwanstein
Guided tours daily April to September 9am to 5.30pm; October to March 10am to 4pm.

Schwangau
Wallfahrtskirche St Colomann
Mid-May to mid-October daily 2.30pm to 4.30pm.

Schongau
Stadtmuseum
Tuesday to Sunday 10am to 12noon and 2pm to 5pm.

Epfach
Museum Abodiacum
April to September daily 10am to 6pm; October to March Saturday and Sunday 10am to 4pm.

Landsberg am Lech
Bayertor
May to September daily 10am to 12noon and 2pm to 5pm.

Rathaus
May to October Monday to Friday 8am to 6pm, Saturday, Sunday and holidays 10am to 12noon and 2pm to 5pm; November to April Monday to Wednesday 8am to 12noon and 2pm to 5pm, Thursday 8am to 12noon and 2pm to 5.30pm, Friday 8am to 12.30pm.

Neues Stadtmuseum
April to January Tuesday to Sunday 2pm to 5pm.

Herkomer-Museum and Mutterturm
April to January Tuesday to Sunday 2pm to 5pm.

Friedberg
Heimatmuseum
Wednesday 2pm to 4pm, Sunday 2pm to 5pm.

Augsburg
Rathaus
Daily 10am to 6pm.

Perlachturm
April to mid-October daily 10am to 6pm.

Maximilianmuseum
May to September Tuesday to Sunday 10am to 5pm; October to April Wednesday to Sunday 10am to 4pm.

Lutherstiege
Tuesday to Sunday 10am to 12noon and 3pm to 5pm.

Schaezler-Palais & Staatsgalerie
May to September Tuesday to Sunday 10am to 5pm; October to
April Wednesday to Sunday 10am to 4pm.

Römisches Museum
May to September Tuesday to Sunday 10am to 5pm; October to
April Wednesday to Sunday 10am to 4pm.

Schwäbischer Handwerkermuseum
Monday and Tuesday 9am to 12noon and 2pm to 6pm, Wednesday
to Friday 2pm to 6pm, Sunday and holidays 10am to 6pm.

Bertolt-Brecht-Haus
May to September Tuesday to Sunday 10am to 5pm; October to
April Wednesday to Sunday 10am to 4pm.

Fuggereimuseum
March to October daily 9am to 6pm.

Mozarthaus
Monday, Wednesday and Thursday 10am to 12noon and 2pm to
5pm, Friday 10am to 12noon and 2pm to 4pm, Saturday and Sunday
10am to 12noon.

Synagoge
Tuesday to Friday 10am to 3pm, Sunday 10am to 5pm.

Gersthofen
Ballon-Museum
 Wednesday 2pm to 6pm, Saturday, Sunday and holidays 10am to
6pm.

Donauwörth
Haus der Stadtgeschichte
Saturday, Sunday and holidays 2pm to 5pm.

Heimatmuseum
Saturday, Sunday and holidays 2pm to 5pm.

Archäologisches Museum
Saturday, Sunday and holidays 2pm to 5pm.

Käthe-Kruse-Puppen-Museum
April to October Tuesday to Sunday 2pm to 5pm; November to
March Wednesday, Saturday, Sunday and holidays 2pm to 5pm.

Harburg

Schloss
Guided tours 16th March to 30th September Tuesday to Sunday 9am to 5pm; 1st to 31st October Tuesday to Sunday 9.30am to 4.30pm.

Kunstsammlung
16th March to 31st October Tuesday to Sunday 10am to 12noon and 2pm to 5pm.

Nördlingen

Löpsinger Tor & Stadtmauermuseum
1st May to 15th October Friday, Saturday and Sunday 10am to 12noon and 1.30pm to 4.30pm.

St Georg
Easter to October Tuesday to Sunday 10am to 12noon and 2pm to 4pm; November to Easter Tuesday to Sunday 11.30am to 12noon.

Danielturm
Daily 9am to dusk.

Stadtmuseum
Easter to mid-October Tuesday to Sunday 10am to 12noon and 1.30pm to 4.30pm.

Rieskrater-Museum
Tuesday to Sunday 10am to 12noon and 1.30pm to 4.30pm.

Bayerisches Eiesenbahnmuseum
April to October Sunday 10am to 5pm.

Wallerstein

Schloss
Guided tours 16th March to 30th September Tuesday to Sunday 9am to 5pm; 1st to 31st October Tuesday to Sunday 9.30am to 4.30pm.

Reitschule
Guided tours 16th March to 30th September Tuesday to Sunday 9am to 5pm; 1st to 31st October Tuesday to Sunday 9.30am to 4.30pm.

Maihingen
Rieser Bauernmuseum
Mid-April to mid-October Tuesday to Thursday, Saturday and Sunday 1pm to 5pm.

Dinkelsbühl
Museum 3. Dimension
April to October daily 10am to 6pm; November to March Saturday and Sunday 11am to 4pm.

Historisches Museum
March to November Tuesday to Sunday 9.30am to 12noon and 1pm to 5pm; December to February Tuesday to Sunday 10am to 12noon and 2pm to 4pm.

Feuchtwangen
Handwerkerstuben
May to October Saturday and Sunday 10am to 12noon and 2pm to 4pm.

Fränkisches Museum
March, November and December Tuesday to Sunday 10am to 12noon and 2pm to 5pm; April to October Tuesday to Sunday 10am to 12noon and 2pm to 6pm.

Zumhaus
Fahrradmuseum
May to September daily 10am to 5pm.

Schillingsfürst
Schloss
Guided tours June to September daily 9am to 11.30am and 2pm to 5.30pm; Easter to 31st May and October Saturday, Sunday and holidays 9am to 11.30am and 2pm to 5.30pm.

Bayerischer Jagdfalkenhof
Daily 10am to 6pm; demonstrations of free flight March to October at 11am and 3pm, May to August also at 5pm.

Brunnenhaus
Easter to October Tuesday to Sunday 10am to 12noon and 2.30pm to 5pm.

Rothenburg ob der Tauber

Rathausturm
April to October daily 9.30am to 12.30pm and 1pm to 4pm; November
to March Saturday and Sunday 12noon to 3pm.

Historiengewölbe
Mid-March to 31st October daily 9am to 6pm.

Puppen- und Spielzeugmuseum
Daily March to December 9.30am to 6pm; January and February
11am to 5pm.

Franziskanerkirche
Monday to Saturday 10am to 12noon and 2pm to 4pm, Sunday 2pm
to 4pm.

St Jakob
Daily Easter to October 9am to 5pm; November to Easter 10am to
12noon and 2pm to 4pm.

Reichstadtmuseum
Daily April to October 10am to 5pm; November to March 1pm to
4pm.

Bauerliches Museum
Easter to October daily 10am to 6pm.

St Wolfgang
March to October daily 10am to 12noon and 2pm to 6pm.

Alt-Rothenburger Handwerkerhaus
Easter to October daily 9am to 6pm.

Mittelalteriches Kriminalmuseum
Daily March 10am to 4pm; April to October 9.30am to 6pm;
November to February 2pm to 4pm.

Rödertor
April to October daily 9am to 5pm.

Topplerschlösschen
Guided tours Friday to Sunday 1pm to 4pm.

Detwang

St Peter und Paul
April, May and 15th September to 31st October daily 8.30am to

12noon and 1.30pm to 5pm; 1st June to 14th September daily 8.30am to 12noon and 1.30pm to 6pm; November to March Tuesday to Sunday 10am to 12noon and 2pm to 4pm.

Creglingen
Herrgottskirche
1st April to 1st November daily 9.15am to 5.30pm; 2nd November to 31st March Tuesday to Sunday 10am to 12noon and 2pm to 4pm.

Fingerhutmuseum
Daily April to October 9am to 6pm; November to March 1pm to 4pm.

Frauental
Kloster
March to October Tuesday to Sunday 10am to 12noon and 2pm to 5pm.

Weikersheim
Tauberländer Dorfmuseum
April to October Tuesday to Sunday 10am to 12noon and 2pm to 5pm.

Schloss
Daily April to October 9am to 6pm; November to March 10am to 12noon and 1.30pm to 4.30pm.

Bad Mergentheim
Schlossmuseum
Tuesday to Friday 2.30pm to 5.30pm, Saturday and Sunday 10am to 12noon and 2pm to 5pm.

Wildpark
March to October daily 9am to 6pm; November to February Saturday, Sunday and holidays 10.30am to 5pm.

Stuppach
Pfarrkirche
Daily March and April 10am to 5pm; May to October 9am to 5.30pm; November to February 11am to 4pm.

Lauda
Heimatmuseum
April to October Sunday 3pm to 5pm.

Tauberbischofsheim
Tauberfränkisches Landschaftsmusuem
Easter to 31st October Tuesday to Saturday 2.30pm to 4.30pm,
Sunday 10am to 12noon and 2.30pm to 4.30pm.

Würzburg
Mainfränkisches Museum
April to October Tuesday to Sunday 10am to 5pm; November to
March Tuesday to Sunday 10am to 4pm.

Fürstenbaumuseum
April to September Tuesday to Sunday 9am to 12.30pm and 1pm to
5pm; October to March Tuesday to Sunday 10am to 12.30pm and
1pm to 4pm.

Marmelsteiner-Kabinett
Tuesday to Friday 2pm to 5pm, Saturday 10am to 12noon, Sunday
10am to 12noon and 2pm to 5pm.

Residenz
April to October Tuesday to Sunday 9am to 5pm; November to
March Tuesday to Sunday 10am to 4pm.

Hofkirche
April to October Tuesday to Sunday 9am to 12noon and 1pm to
5pm; November to March Tuesday to Sunday 10am to 12noon and
1pm to 4pm.

Martin-von-Wagner-Museum
Tuesday to Saturday 9.30am to 12.30pm and 2pm to 5pm, Sunday
9.30am to 12.30pm.

2: Some Useful Words and Phrases

English is a compulsory subject in German schools, hence many Germans have a good command of the language. However, many others, particularly in rural areas, do not, and it therefore helps to know at least a little German. The following is a list of words and phrases likely to be of most use when travelling along the Romantic Road.

ON THE ROUTE

Marked hiking path	der Wanderweg
Footpath	der Fussweg
Cycle path	der Radweg
Farm track	der Wirtschaftsweg
Forest Path	der Waldweg
Road, street	die Strasse
Steps	die Treppe
Meadow	die Wiese
Field	die Weide
Forest	der Wald
River	der Fluss
Stream, brook	der Bach
Lake	der See
Dam	die Talsperre
Valley	das Tal
Hill	der Hügel
Mountain	der Berg
Mill	die Mühle
Picnic area, layby	das Rastplatz
Viewpoint	der Aussichtspunkt
Village	das Dorf
Town, city	die Stadt
North	Nord
South	Süd
East	Ost
West	West
Right	Rechts
Left	Links

Straight ahead	Gerade aus
Entrance	Eingang
No entrance	Kein Eingang
Exit	Ausgang
Attention!	Achtung!
Beware!	Vorsicht!
Prohibited	Verboten
Open	Geöffnet, Offen, Auf
Closed	Geschlossen, Zu
Please	Bitte
Thank you very much	Danke schön
Excuse me	Entschuldigen Sie mir bitte
Do you speak English?	Sprechen Sie Englisch?
Can you help me?	Können Sie mir helfen?
How do I get to ...?	Wie komme ich nach ...?
How far is it to ...?	Wie weit ist es von hier nach ...?
Is this the way to ...?	Ist das der Weg nach ...?
Where is ...?	Wo ist ...?
What time is it?	Wie spät ist es?

DAYS, TIMES AND GREETINGS

Monday	Montag
Tuesday	Dienstag
Wednesday	Mittwoch
Thursday	Donnerstag
Friday	Freitag
Saturday	Samstag
Sunday	Sonntag
Today	Heute
Yesterday	Gestern
Tomorrow	Morgen
In the morning	Am Vormittag
In the afternoon	Am Nachmittag
In the evening	Am Abend
Good morning	Guten Morgen
Good day	Guten Tag, Grüss Gott
Good evening	Guten Abend
How are you?	Wie geht es Ihnen?

Goodbye	Auf Wiedersehen
Goodbye (informal)	Tschüs
Yes	Ja
No	Nein

COMMUNICATIONS AND TRANSPORT

Map	die Landkarte
Town plan	der Stadtplan
Tourist office	das Verkehrsamt
Post office	das Postamt
Postcard	die Postkarte
Postage stamp	die Briefmarke
Bank	die Bank
Currency exchange	die Geldwechsel
Travellers' cheque	der Reisescheck
Passport	der Reisepass
Bicycle	das Fahrrad
Train	der Zug, die Bahn
Station	der Bahnhof
Platform	der Bahnsteig
Left luggage	die Gepäckabfertigung
Left luggage locker	das Schliessfach
Bus	der Bus
Bus stop	die Bushaltestelle
Cable car	die Seilbahn
Tram	die Strassenbahn
Car	das Auto
Petrol	das Benzin
Journey	die Reise
Ticket	die Fahrkarte, der Fahrschein
Single	Einfach
Return	Hin-und-Zurück
Timetable	der Fahrplan
Departure	die Abfahrt
Arrival	die Ankunft

What is the fare to ...?	Wieviel kostet es nach ...?
When does the next bus leave?	Wann fährt der nächste Bus?

From which platform does the train leave?	Von welchen Bahnsteig fährt der Zug?

SIGHTSEEING

Church	die Kirche
Parish church	die Pfarrkirche
Pilgrimage church	die Wallfahrtskirche
Chapel	die Kapelle
Cathedral	der Dom
Monastery, Convent	das Kloster
Town hall	das Rathaus
Town wall	die Stadtmauer
Gateway	das Tor
Tower	der Turm
Bridge	die Brücke
Fortress	die Festung
Castle (fortified)	die Burg
Castle (stately home)	das Schloss
Residential palace	die Residenz, das Palais
Fountain	der Brunnen

ACCOMMODATION

Inn	der Gasthof, das Gasthaus
Room	das Zimmer
Rooms free	Zimmer frei
Bed	das Bett
Key	die Schlüssel
Bath	das Bad
Shower	die Dusche
Toilet	die Toilette
Ladies	Damen
Gentlemen	Herren
Vacant	Frei
Occupied	Besetzt
Lift, elevator	der Fahrstuhl
Telephone	das Telephon
Television	das Fernsehen
I have reserved a room	Ich habe ein Zimmer reserviert

Are there rooms available?	Haben Sie Zimmer frei?
I'd like a single (double) room	Ich hätte gern ein Einzelzimmer (Doppelzimmer)
Does it have a shower (bath, toilet)?	Hat es Dusche (Bad, Toilette)?
How much does it cost?	Wieviel kostet es?
At what time is breakfast served?	Um wieviel Uhr wird das Frühstück serviert?

FOOD AND DRINK

Breakfast	das Frühstück
Lunch	das Mittagessen
Dinner	das Abendessen
Knife	das Messer
Fork	die Gabel
Spoon	der Löffel
Plate	der Teller
Bread	das Brot
Bread roll	das Brötchen
Salt	das Salz
Pepper	der Pfeffer
Sugar	der Zucker
Jam	die Marmelade
Honey	der Honig
Butter	die Butter
Cheese	die Käse
Cream	die Sahne
Egg	das Ei
Starter	die Vorspeise
Soup	die Suppe
Main course	das Hauptgericht
Fish	der Fisch
Beef	das Rindfleisch
Pork	das Schweinefleisch
Veal	das Kalbfleisch
Venison	das Rehfleisch
Lamb	das Lammfleisch
Chicken	das Hähnchen, das Huhn
Vegetable	das Gemüse

Potato	die Kartoffel
Salad	der Salat
Fruit	das Obst
Dessert	die Nachspeise
Gateau	die Torte
Cake	der Kuchen
Chocolate	die Schockolade
Biscuit	der Keks
Water	das Wasser
Mineral water	das Mineralwasser
Milk	das Milch
Beer	das Bier
Draught beer	das Fassbier
Red wine	der Rotwein
White wine	der Weisswein
Sparkling wine	der Sekt
Cider	der Apfelwein
Liqueur	der Likör
Apple juice	der Apfelsaft
Grape juice	der Traubensaft
Orange juice	der Orangensaft
Lemonade	die Zitronenlimonade
Coffee	der Kaffee
Cocoa	der Kakao
Tea	der Tee
Herbal tea	der Kräutertee, der Pflanzentee
Glass	das Glas
Bottle	die Flasche
Is this seat/place free?	Ist diese Platz frei?
The menu, please	Die Speisekarte bitte
The bill, please	Die Rechnung bitte
Where are the toilets?	Wo sind die Toiletten?

EMERGENCIES

Police	die Polizei
Doctor	der Arzt
Dentist	der Zahnarzt
Chemist	die Apotheke

Hospital	das Krankenhaus
Ambulance	der Krankenwagen
Insurance	die Versicherung
Accident	der Unfall
Allergy	die Allergie
Pain	der Schmerz
Lost	Verloren
Stolen	Gestohlen
Help!	Hilfe!

I have a headache (stomach ache, toothache, a cold)	Ich habe Kopfschmerzen (Magenschmerzen, Zahnweh, Schnupfen)

NUMBERS

One	Eins	Sixteen	Sechzehn
Two	Zwei	Seventeen	Siebzehn
Three	Drei	Eighteen	Achtzehn
Four	Vier	Nineteen	Neunzehn
Five	Fünf	Twenty	Zwanzig
Six	Sechs	Thirty	Dreissig
Seven	Sieben	Forty	Vierzig
Eight	Acht	Fifty	Fünfzig
Nine	Neun	Sixty	Sechzig
Ten	Zehn	Seventy	Siebzig
Eleven	Elf	Eighty	Achtzig
Twelve	Zwölf	Ninety	Neunzig
Thirteen	Dreizehn	Hundred	Hundert
Fourteen	Vierzehn	Thousand	Tausend
Fifteen	Fünfzehn		

3: Tourist Offices

Kurverwaltung,
Kaiser-Maximilian-Platz 1,
87629 Füssen
Tel: (0 83 62) 70 77

Kurverwaltung,
Münchener Strasse 2,
87645 Schwangau
Tel: (0 83 62) 8 19 80

Verkehrsamt,
Schongauer Strasse 1,
86989 Steingaden
Tel: (0 88 62) 2 00

Verkehrsverein,
Kirchbergstrasse 20a,
82409 Wildsteig
Tel: (0 88 67) 4 09

Verkehrsverein,
Klosterhof 36,
82401 Rottenbuch
Tel: (0 88 67) 14 64

Verkehrsverein,
Ammergauer Strasse 2,
86971 Peiting
Tel: (0 88 61) 65 35

Verkehrsamt,
Münzstrasse 5,
86956 Schongau
Tel: (0 88 61) 72 16

Tourist-Information,
Lechstrasse 4,
86978 Hohenfurch
Tel: (00 88 61) 44 23

Kultur-und
Fremdenverkehrsamt,
Hauptplatz 1,
86899 Landsberg am Lech
Tel: (0 81 91) 12 82 46

Fremdenverkehrsbüro,
Marienplatz 14,
86316 Friedberg
Tel: (08 21) 6 00 22 13

Tourist-Information,
Bahnhofstrasse 7,
86150 Augsburg
Tel: (08 21) 5 02 07-0

Tourist-Information
Rathausplatz,
86150 Augsburg
Tel: (08 21) 5 02 07-24

Tourist-Information,
Rathausgasse 1,
86609 Donauwörth
Tel: (09 06) 78 91 45

Stadtverwaltung,
Schloss Strasse 1,
86655 Harburg
Tel: (0 90 03) 9 69 90

Verkehrsamt,
Marktplatz 2,
86720 Nördlingen
Tel: (0 90 81) 43 80

Marktgemeindeverwaltung,
Weinstrasse 19,
86757 Wallerstein
Tel: (0 90 81) 70 35

Tourist-Information,
Marktplatz 1,
91550 Dinkelsbühl
Tel: (0 98 51) 9 02 40

Kultur- und Verkehrsamt,
Marktplatz 1,
91555 Feuchtwangen
Tel: (0 98 52) 9 04 44

Städtisches Verkehrsamt,
Anton-Roth-Weg 9,
91583 Schillingsfürst
Tel: (0 98 68) 8 00

Kultur- und
Fremdenverkehrsamt,
Marktplatz 2,
91541 Rothenburg ob der
Tauber
Tel: (0 98 61) 4 04 92

Touristikzentrum Oberes
Taubertal,
An der Romantischen Strasse 14,
97993 Creglingen
Tel: (0 79 33) 6 31

Verkehrsamt,
Marktplatz 1,
97285 Röttingen
Tel: (0 93 38) 2 00

Städtisches Kultur- und
Verkehrsamt,
Marktplatz 7,
97990 Weikersheim
Tel: (0 79 34) 1 02 55

Städtisches Kultur- und
Verkehrsamt,
Marktplatz 3,
97980 Bad Mergentheim
Tel: (0 79 31) 5 71 35

Kurverwaltung,
Lothar-Daiker-Strasse 4,
97980 Bad Mergentheim
Tel: (0 79 31) 54 95 22

Kultur- und Verkehrsamt,
Marktplatz 1,
97922 Lauda
Tel: (0 93 43) 50 10

Verkehrsamt,
Marktplatz 8,
97941 Tauberbischofsheim
Tel: (0 93 41) 8 03 13

Congress & Tourismus Zentrale,
Am Congress Centrum,
97070 Würzburg
Tel: (09 31) 3 73 35

Tourist-Information,
Pavillon am Hauptbahnhof,
97070 Würzburg
Tel: (09 31) 3 74 36

Tourist-Information,
Haus zum Falken,
Marktplatz,
97070 Würzburg
Tel: (09 31) 3 73 98

4: List of Accommodation

Hotels, Inns and Pensions

In the first column of the list below, H stands for Hotel, HG for Hotel Garni, HP for Hotel-Pension, G for Gasthof, P for Pension. As far as it is possible to do so, the entries under each town are listed in descending order of price. The gradings (E), (M) and (B) at the end of each entry signify expensive, moderate and budget respectively. However these are intended as a rough guide only: many hotels have rooms available at widely differing rates, according to whether or not they have such facilities as en suite bathrooms, cable televisions, or balconies with panoramic views.

Note that many establishments, particularly those located in smaller villages, close for one day each week. Advance reservations (even if made only a day or two beforehand) are strongly recommended, particularly for places where accommodation provision is sparse.

Füssen

H	Hirsch, Kaiser-Maximilian-Platz 7, Tel: (0 83 62) 50 80 (M)
H	Sonne, Reichenstrasse 37, Tel: (0 83 62) 60 61 (M)
HP	Landhaus Sommer am See, Weidachstrasse 74, Tel: (0 83 62) 76 46 (M)
H	Zum Hechten, Ritterstrasse 6, Tel: (0 83 62) 79 06 (M)
HG	Elisabeth, Augustenstrasse 10, Tel: (0 83 62) 62 75 (B)
HP	Haus am Forggensee, Weidachstrasse 39, Tel: (0 83 62) 36 36 (B)
P	Berktold, Säulingstrasse 2, Tel: (0 83 62) 65 05 (B)

Hohenschwangau

H	Schlosshotel Lisl und Jägerhaus, Neuschwansteinstrasse 1-3, Tel: (0 83 62) 88 70 (E)
H	Seehotel Alpenrose, Alpseestrasse 27, Tel: (0 83 62) 88 60 (E)
H	Alpenstuben, Alpseestrasse 8, Tel: (0 83 62) 8 12 14 (M)
H	Schlossblick, Schwangauer Strasse 7, Tel: (0 83 62) 8 11 65 (B)

Schwangau

H	König Ludwig, Kreuzweg 11, Tel: (0 83 62) 8 89-0 (E)
H	Weinbauer, Füssener Strasse 3, Tel: (0 83 62) 8 10 15 (M)
G	Post, Münchener Strasse 5, Tel: (0 83 62) 82 35 (M)

G   Hanselewirt, Mitteldorf 13, Tel: (0 83 62) 82 37 (B)
P   Schlossblick, Füssener Strasse 48, Tel: (0 83 62) 83 55 (B)

Buching
H   Bannwaldsee, Sesselbahnstrasse 10, Tel: (0 83 68) 8 51 (E)
G   Geiselstein, Füssener Strasse 26, Tel: (0 83 68) 2 60 (M)
G   Schäder, Romantische Strasse 16, Tel: (0 83 68) 13 40 (M)

Trauchgau
H   Sonnenbichl, Am Müllerbichl 1, Tel: (0 83 68) 8 71 (M)

Wies
G   Moser, Wies 1, Tel: (0 88 62) 5 03 (B)

Steingaden
G   Lindenhof, Schongauer Strasse 35, Tel: (0 88 62) 60 11 (M)
G   Graf, Schongauer Strasse 15, Tel: (0 88 62) 2 46 (B)
G   Zur Post, Marktplatz 1, Tel: (0 88 62) 2 03 (B)

Wildsteig
G   Strauss, Riedstrasse 16, Tel: (0 88 67) 3 72 (B)

Rottenbuch
H   Moosbeck-Alm, Moos 38, Tel: (0 88 67) 13 47 (M)
H   Café am Tor, Klosterhof 1, Tel: (0 88 67) 2 55 (M)
P   Mayer, Vogelherd 7, Tel: (0 88 67) 2 23 (B)

Peiting
H   Dragoner, Ammergauer Strasse 11, Tel: (0 88 61) 60 51 (M)
H   Zum Pinzger, Am Hauptplatz 9, Tel: (0 88 61) 62 40 (M)
G   Zum Buchberger, Füssener Strasse 2, Tel: (0 88 61) 62 66 (M)
G   Keppeler, Am Hauptplatz 15, Tel: (0 88 61) 62 01 (M)

Schongau
HG Rössle, Christophstrasse 49, Tel: (0 88 61) 2 30 50 (M)
H   Holl, Altenstädter Strasse 39, Tel: (0 88 61) 40 51 (M)
H   Alte Post, Marienplatz 19, Tel: (0 88 61) 23 20-0 (M)
H   Blaue Traube, Münzstrasse 10, Tel: (0 88 61) 9 03 29 (M)
G   Sonne, Lindenplatz 13, Tel: (0 88 61) 72 75 (B)

Hohenfurch

G   Schönachhof, Kapellenstrasse 22, Tel: (0 88 61) 41 08 (B)
G   Negele, Hauptplatz 2, Tel: (0 88 61) 44 63 (B)
P   Gerbl, Lechstrasse 4, Tel: (0 88 61) 44 23 (B)

Landsberg am Lech

H   Goggl, Herkomerstrasse 19-20, Tel: (0 89 91) 32 40 (E)
H   Landsberger Hof, Weilheimer Strasse 5, Tel: (0 89 91) 3 20 20 (M)
G   Zum Mohren, Hauptplatz 148, Tel: (0 81 91) 4 22 10 (M)
P   Landhotel Endhart, Erpftinger Strasse 19, Tel: (0 81 91) 9 20 74 (M)
P   Gästehaus Christine, Galgenweg 4, Tel: (0 81 91) 52 10 (B)

Friedberg

HG Zum Brunnen, Bauernbräustrasse 4, Tel: (08 21) 60 30 23 (E)
G   Café Frey, Münchner Strasse 11, Tel: (08 21) 60 50 61-2 (M)
G   Kreisi, Hergottsruhstrasse 18, Tel: (08 21) 2 67 90 00 (B)
G   Stefanshof, Stefanstrasse 4, Tel: (08 21) 60 23 17 (B)

Augsburg

H   Drei Mohren, Maximilianstrasse 40, Tel: (08 21) 5 03 60 (E)
H   Augusta, Ludwigstrasse 2, Tel: (08 21) 5 01 40 (E)
HG Altstadthotel Ulrich, Kapuzinergasse 6, Tel: (08 21) 3 30 77 (E)
HG Dom-Hotel, Frauentorstrasse 8, Tel: (08 21) 15 30 31 (E)
H   Fischertor, Pfärrle 16, Tel: (08 21) 15 60 51 (M)
H   Jakoberhof, Jakoberstrasse 39-41, Tel: (08 21) 51 00 30 (M)
HG Georgsrast, Georgenstrasse 31, Tel: (08 21) 50 26 10 (M)
HG Iris, Gartenstrasse 4, Tel: (08 21) 51 09 81 (M)
HP Linderhof, Aspernstrasse 38, Tel: (08 21) 71 30 16 (B)
G   Lenzhalde, Thelottstrasse 2, Tel: (08 21) 52 07 45 (B)
P   Bayerischer Löwe, Linke Brandstrasse 2, Tel: (08 21) 74 25 79 (B)
P   Märkl, Schillstrasse 20, Tel: (08 21) 79 14 99 (B)

Donauwörth

H   Posthotel Traube, Kapellstrasse 14-16, Tel: (09 06) 60 96 (E)
G   Goldener Greifen, Pflegstrasse 15, Tel: (09 06) 33 75 (B)
G   Goldener Hirsch, Reichsstrasse 44, Tel: (09 06) 31 24 (B)
G   Feuerle, Heilig-Kreuz-Strasse 4, Tel: (09 06) 37 33 (B)

P   Haus Gertrud, Johann-Traber-Strasse 5, Tel: (09 06) 57 20 (B)
P   Graf, Zirgesheimer Strasse 5, Tel: (09 06) 51 17 (B)

Harburg
H   Fürstliche Burgschenke, Burgstrasse 1, Tel: (09 03) 15 04 (M)
G   Goldenes Lamm, Marktplatz 15, Tel: (09 03) 14 22 (B)
G   Zum Straussen, Marktplatz 2, Tel: (09 03) 13 98 (B)

Nördlingen
H   Klösterle, Beim Klösterle 1, Tel: (0 90 81) 8 80 54 (E)
H   Sonne, Marktplatz 3, Tel: (0 90 81) 50 67 (M)
HG   Goldene Rose, Baldinger Strasse 42, Tel: (0 90 81) 8 60 19 (M)
G   Zum Engel, Wemdinger Strasse 4, Tel: (0 90 81) 31 67 (M)
HG   Altreuter, Marktplatz 11, Tel: (0 90 81) 43 19 (B)
G   Goldenes Lamm, Schäfflesmarkt 3, Tel: (0 90 81) 2 87 49 (B)
G   Walfisch, Hallgasse 15, Tel: (0 90 81) 31 07 (B)
G   Drei Mohren, Reimlinger Strasse 18, Tel: (0 90 81) 31 13 (B)

Wallerstein
G   Zum Goldenen Löwen, Obere Bergstrasse 1, Tel: (0 90 81) 71 08 (B)

Maihingen
G   Zur Goldenen Sonne, Am Dorfplatz, Tel: (0 90 87) 2 26 (B)

Dinkelsbühl
H   Deutsches Haus, Weinmarkt 3, Tel: (0 98 51) 60 58 (M)
H   Eisenkrug, Dr-Martin-Luther-Strasse 1, Tel: (0 98 51) 5 77 00 (M)
H   Blauer Hecht, Schweinemarkt 1, Tel: (0 98 51) 8 11 (M)
H   Goldene Rose, Marktplatz 4, Tel: (0 98 51) 5 77 50 (M)
H   Goldene Kanne, Segringer Strasse 8, Tel: (0 98 51) 60 11 (M)
G   Goldener Anker, Untere Schmiedgasse 22, Tel: (0 98 51) 5 78 00 (M)
G   Weisses Ross, Steingasse 12, Tel: (0 98 51) 22 74 (M)
P   Lutz, Schäfergässlein 4, Tel: (0 98 51) 94 54 (B)
P   Gerda, Nestleinsberg 24, Tel: (0 98 51) 18 60 (B)

Feuchtwangen

H Greifen-Post, Marktplatz 8, Tel: (0 98 52) 68 00 (E)
G Lamm, Marktplatz 5, Tel: (0 98 52) 25 00 (M)
G Wilder Mann, Alter Ansbacher Berg 2, Tel: (0 98 52) 7 19 (M)
G Sindel-Buchel, Spitalstrasse 28, Tel: (0 98 52) 25 94 (M)
G Ballheimer, Ringstrasse 57, Tel: (0 98 52) 91 82 (M)
G Fränkischer Hof, Am Bahnhof 10, Tel: (0 98 52) 23 30 (B)

Schillingsfürst

H Die Post, Rothenburger Strasse 1, Tel: (0 98 68) 4 73 (M)
H Zapf, Dombühler Strasse 7-9, Tel: (0 98 68) 50 20 (M)
G Adler, Am Markt 8, Tel: (0 98 68) 14 11 (M)

Faulenberg

G Zur Waldesruh, Faulenberg 19, Tel: (0 98 68) 57 25 (B)

Rothenburg ob der Tauber

H   Eisenhut, Herrngasse 3-7, Tel: (0 98 61) 70 50 (E)
H   Goldener Hirsch, Untere Schmiedgasse 16, Tel: (0 98 61) 70 80 (E)
H   Bären, Hofbronnengasse 7-9, Tel: (0 98 61) 9 44 10 (E)
H   Roter Hahn, Obere Schmiedgasse 21, Tel: (0 98 61) 50 88 (M)
H   Glocke, Am Plönlein 1, Tel: (0 98 61) 30 25 (M)
HP Spitzweg, Paradeisgasse 2, Tel: (0 98 61) 60 61 (M)
HP Café Gerberhaus, Spitalgasse 25, Tel: (0 98 61) 9 49 00 (M)
G   Linde, Vorm Würzburger Tor 12, Tel: (0 98 61) 74 44 (M)
G   Zum Greifen, Obere Schmiedgasse 5, Tel: (0 98 61) 22 81 (B)
G   Goldene Rose, Spitalgasse 28, Tel: (0 98 61) 46 38 (B)
P   Gästehaus Raidel, Wenggasse 3, Tel: (0 98 61) 31 15 (B)
P   Pöschel, Wenggasse 22, Tel: (0 98 61) 34 30 (B)

Creglingen

G Krone, Hauptstrasse 12, Tel: (0 79 33) 5 58 (M)
G Herrgottstal, Herrgottstal 13, Tel: (0 79 33) 5 18 (M)
G Grüner Baum, Torstrasse 20, Tel: (0 79 33) 6 18 (B)

Weidenhof

P Stahl (Heuhotel), Tel: (0 79 33) 3 78

Klingen
G   Zur Romantischen Strasse, Klingen 28, Tel: (0 93 38) 2 09 (B)

Bieberehren
G   Zum Adler, Hauptstrasse 19, Tel: (0 93 38) 3 51 (B)

Röttingen
H   Rebstöckle, Rothenburger Strasse 2, Tel: (0 93 38) 5 31 (M)
G   Zum Ochsen, Marktplatz 6, Tel: (0 93 38) 2 72 (B)

Tauberrettersheim
H   Krone, Mühlenstrasse 6, Tel: (0 93 38) 4 12 (M)
G   Zum Hirschen, Mühlenstrasse 1, Tel: (0 93 38) 3 22 (M)

Weikersheim
H   Laurentius, Marktplatz 5, Tel: (0 79 34) 70 07 (M)
H   Grüner Hof, Marktplatz 10, Tel: (0 79 34) 2 52 (M)
H   Deutschherren-Stuben, Marktplatz 9, Tel: (0 79 34) 83 76 (B)
G   Zur Krone, Hauptstrasse 24, Tel: (0 79 34) 83 14 (B)

Markelsheim
H   Weinstube Lochner, Hauptstrasse 39, Tel: (0 79 31) 20 81 (M)
HG Gästehaus Birgit, Scheuerntorstrasse 25, Tel: (0 79 31) 9 09 00 (M)

Igersheim
G   Zum Löwen, Goldbachstrasse 8, Tel: (0 79 31) 25 90 (B)
G   Tauberbrücke, Bad Mergentheimer Strasse 26,
      Tel: (0 79 31) 23 48 (B)

Bad Mergentheim
H   Victoria, Poststrasse 2-4, Tel: (0 79 31) 59 30 (E)
H   Bundschu, Cronbergstrasse 15, Tel: (0 79 31) 30 43 (E)
H   Alte Münze, Munzgasse 12-14, Tel: (0 79 31) 56 60 (M)
H   Deutschmeister, Ochsengasse 7, Tel: (0 79 31) 70 58 (M)
HG Gästehaus am Schloss, Frommengasse 12, Tel: (0 79 31) 61 62 (M)
G   Zum Wilden Mann, Reichengässle 6, Tel: (0 79 31) 76 38 (B)

Königshofen

H   Gemmrig's Landhaus, Hauptstrasse 68, Tel: (0 93 43) 70 51 (M)
G   Rose, Turmbergstrasse 9, Tel: (0 93 43) 13 33 (M)

Lauda

H   Ratskeller, Josef-Schmitt-Strasse 17, Tel: (0 93 43) 6 20 70 (M)
H   Zur Alten Schmiede, Maierstrasse 1-3, Tel: (0 93 43) 9 74 (M)
G   Goldener Stern, Pfarrstrasse 23, Tel: (0 93 43) 12 71 (B)

Distelhausen

G   Grüner Baum, Bundesstrasse 23, Tel: (0 93 41) 24 19 (B)

Dittigheim

G   Zum Grünen Baum, Rathausplatz 1, Tel: (0 93 41) 51 62 (B)

Tauberbischofsheim

H   Am Brenner, Goethestrasse 10, Tel: (0 93 41) 9 21 30 (M)
H   Badischer Hof, Hauptstrasse 70, Tel: (0 93 41) 98 80 (M)
H   Adlerhof, Bahnhofstrasse 18, Tel: (0 93 41) 23 36 (M)
H   Am Schloss, Hauptstrasse 56, Tel: (0 93 41) 32 71 (M)
P   Stein, Hauptstrasse 67, Tel: (0 93 41) 32 04 (B)

Werbach

G   Drei Lilien, Hauptstrasse 14, Tel: (0 93 41) 75 86 (M)
P   Gästehaus Kettner, Liebfrauenbrunnstrasse 12,
Tel: (0 93 41) 29 27 (B)

Würzburg

H   Rebstock, Neubaustrasse 7, Tel: (09 31) 3 09 30 (E)
H   Walfisch, Am Pleidenturm 5, Tel: (09 31) 5 00 55 (E)
H   Zur Stadt Mainz, Semmelstrasse 39, Tel: (09 31) 5 31 55 (E)
HG   Alter Kranen, Kärmergasse 11, Tel: (09 31) 3 51 80 (E)
HG   Zum Winzermännle, Domstrasse 32, Tel: (09 31) 5 41 56 (M)
H   Greifenstein, Häfnergasse 1, Tel: (09 31) 3 51 70 (M)
HG   Schönleber, Theaterstrasse 5, Tel: (09 31) 1 20 68 (M)
H   Franziskaner, Franziskanerplatz 2, Tel: (09 31) 1 50 01 (M)
H   Russ, Wolfhartsgasse 1, Tel: (09 31) 5 00 16 (M)
HG   Luitpoldbrücke, Pleichertorstrasse 26, Tel: (09 31) 5 02 44 (M)

P   Spehnkuch, Röntgenring 7, Tel: (09 31) 5 47 52 (B)
P   Siegel, Reisgrubengasse 7, Tel: (09 31) 5 29 41 (B)

Youth Hostels
Mariahilferstrasse 5, Füssen, Tel: (0 83 62) 77 54
Beim Pfaffenkeller 3, Augsburg, Tel: (08 21) 3 39 09
Goethestrasse 10, Donauwörth, Tel: (09 06) 51 58
Kaiserwiese 1, Nördlingen, Tel: (0 90 81) 8 41 09
Koppengasse 10, Dinkelsbühl, Tel: (0 98 51) 95 09
Mühlacker 1, Rothenburg ob der Tauber, Tel: (0 98 61) 45 10
Erdbacher Strasse 10, Creglingen, Tel: (0 79 33) 3 36
Im Heiligen Wöhr, Weikersheim, Tel: (0 79 34) 70 25
Erlenbachtalstrasse 44, Igersheim, Tel: (0 79 31) 63 73
Schirrmannweg 2, Tauberbischofsheim, Tel: (0 93 41) 31 52
Burkarderstrasse 44, Würzburg, Tel: (09 31) 4 25 90

Campsites
Campingplatz Hopfensee, Hopfen am See, Tel: (0 83 62) 74 31
Ferienplatz Brunnen, Seestrasse 81, Schwangau, Tel: (0 83 62) 82 73
Campingplatz Bannwaldsee, Münchener Strasse 151, Schwangau,
    Tel: (0 83 62) 8 10 01
Terrassencamping am Richterbichl, Solder 1, Rottenbuch,
    Tel: (0 88 67) 15 00
Campingpark Romantik am Lech, Am Pössinger Wald, Landsberg
    am Lech, Tel: (0 81 91) 4 75 05
Campingplatz Ludwigshof, Ludwigshof am See, Tel: (0 82 07) 10 77
Campingplatz Augusta, Mülhauser Strasse 54, Augsburg,
    Tel: (08 21) 79 58 83
Donau-Lech-Camping, Campingweg 1, Egglestetten,
    Tel: (09 02) 40 44
Campingplatz Romantische Strasse, Dürrwanger Strasse,
    Dinkelsbühl, Tel: (0 98 51) 78 17
Campingplatz Frankenhöhe, Am Fischaus, Schillingsfürst,
    Tel: (0 98 68) 51 11
Campingplatz Tauber-Romantik, Detwang, Tel: (0 98 61) 61 91

Campingplatz Tauber-Idyll, Detwang, Tel: (0 98 61) 31 77

Campingplatz Romantische Strasse, Creglingen-Münster,
Tel: (0 79 33) 3 21

Campingplatz Willinger Tal, Bad Mergentheim, Tel: (0 79 31) 21 77

Campingplatz Kalte Quelle, Winterhäuser Strasse 160, Würzburg,
Tel: (09 31) 3 73 35

5: Festivals

Füssen
Furstensaalkonzerte (one week in late May) - a series of concerts of classical music in the Fürstensaal of Kloster St Mang.
Stadtfest (2nd weekend in July) - summer festival.

Hohenschwangau
Schlosskonzerte (one week in mid- to late September) - a series of concerts, including music by Wagner, in the Sängersaal of Schloss Neuschwanstein.

Schwangau
Colomansfest (2nd Sunday in October). Held in honour of the martyred Irish missionary St Coloman, this is the best known of Bavaria's many equestrian religious festivals. It begins with a procession of around 300 horses and riders (including several historic carriages) from the Rathaus to the Wallfahrtskirche St Coloman. An open-air mass is then held, after which the horses are blessed, then ridden round the church three times. Afterwards, beer and food are served from the tents outside.

Wies
The main pilgrimages to the Wieskirche take place on the Sunday after 14th June (the Feast of Christ's Tears), the 1st Sunday in September (the Feast of the Guardian Angel), and the 2nd Sunday in October (the Feast of the Holy Brotherhood).

Steingaden
St-Ulrichs-Ritt (Sunday after 4th July). Held soon after St Urich's Day, this is another equestrian religious festival, featuring a horseback procession to the Heilig-Kreuz-Kirche (Holy Cross Church) on the Kreuzberg, a hill south of the town. On the same weekend, the Stadelfest ("Barn Festival") takes place in the town centre.

Wildsteig
Leonhardiritt (3rd Sunday in October). This is similar to the Colomansfest in Schwangau, though on a smaller scale, with

processions through the village before and after the open-air mass with blessing of the horses.

Rottenbuch
Kaltblutfohlenmarkt (early September). Germany's biggest market for young carthorses is accompanied by tents selling the traditional festival food and beer.
Leonhardiritt (last Sunday in October or 1st Sunday in November). This takes the same form as its counterpart in Wildsteig.

Peiting
Bürgerfest (one week in late July and/or early August) - summer fair.

Schongau
Stadtfest (at Corpus Christi) - the first of two summer fairs.
Volksfest (10 days in late July and/or early August) - the main summer fair.
Christkindlmarkt (throughout Advent) - Christmas market.

Vilgertshofen
Stumme Prozession (15th August). The "Silent Procession" (so called because of the absence of the usual accompanying band) is a costumed procession of tableaux of Old and New Testament scenes. It is followed by an open-air mass to celebrate the Feast of the Assumption.

Landsberg am Lech
Ruethenfest (weekend in late July). Held every four years (1999, 2003, 2007), the "Rod Festival" is one of the biggest children's festivals in Germany. There are two big processions featuring floats, historical tableaux and children bearing the cut-down branches which give the festival its name. The festival also features re-creations of military camps, a handicrafts market, street theatre and open-air concerts.
Stadtfest (Saturday in late July) - a much more modest summer fair held in years when the Ruethenfest does not take place.
Christkindlmarkt (thoughout Advent) - Christmas market.

Friedberg

Historisches Altstadtfest (10 days in late June and early July). Held every three years (1998, 2001, 2004), this re-creates various periods in the town's past.

Volks- und Heimatfest (early August) - summer fair.

Ausburg

Frühjahrsdult (for two weeks from Easter Saturday) - spring fair.

Frühjahrsplärrer (for two weeks from Easter Sunday) spring funfair.

Jakober Kirchweih (10 days in late July and early August) - summer fair with beer tents and funfair.

Friedensfest (8th August). Originally Protestant, but now ecumenical, the "Peace Festival" was first held in 1650 to celebrate the end of the religious conflicts of the Thirty Years' War.

Herbstplärrer (last week in August and first week in September) - autumn funfair.

Augsburger Mozartsommer (two weeks from late August to early September) - candlelit concerts of music by Mozart in the Festsaal of the Schaezler-Palais.

Herbstdult (early October) - autumn fair.

Christkindlesmarkt (throughout Advent). Thanks to continuing to adhere to a traditional approach, this is one of the most prestigious of the Christmas markets which have become a standard feature of almost every German town.

Donauwörth

Schwäbischwerder Kindertag (Sunday in late June or early July) - children's festival with a costumed procession of historical tableaux.

Donauwörther Kulturtage (three weeks in October) - season of concerts, theatre and exhibitions.

Harburg

Brückenfest (weekend in late July) - summer market and fair.

Nördlingen

Stabenfest (2nd Monday in May). The "Staff Festival", which celebrates the arrival of spring, features a parade of children wearing floral wreaths and carrying branches.

Pfingstmesse (10 days from the 2nd Saturday after Whitsun) - Whit fair.

Scharlachrennen (mid-July). The "Scarlet Race" is a revival of a horse race held in the 15th and 16th centuries. Competitors vie for the traditional medieval prize of a piece of scarlet cloth.

Stadtmauerfest (weekend in late September). Held every three years (1999, 2002, 2005), the "Town Wall Festival" is a costumed event with processions.

Wallerstein
Herbstmarkt (2nd Sunday in September) - autumn fair.

Dinkelsbühl
Kinderzech'-Festwoche (10 days around the 3rd Monday in July). This famous festival celebrates an event in the Thirty Years' War, when the local children successfully petitioned the occupying Swedish army to spare the town from destruction. In addition to re-enactments of the event, there are several costumed processions as well as beer tents, a fair, a fireworks display and open-air theatrical performances.

Stadtfest (2nd or 3rd Sunday in September) - autumn fair.

Feuchtwangen
Kreuzgangspiele (June to mid-August) - season of open-air theatrical performances in the Kreuzgang.

Altstadtfest (weekend in mid-June) - summer fair.

Mooswiese (long weekend in late September). In addition to a costumed procession of historical tableaux, the attractions include a beer tent, a funfair and a market.

Rothenburg ob der Tauber
Schäfertanz (selected Sundays in summer). The costumed "Shepherds' Dance", performed on the Marktplatz, has been performed for so long that its origins are obscure: one tradition maintains that it was originally a thanksgiving for Rothenburg's deliverance from the plague, another that it celebrates a shepherd's discovery of treasure.

"Der Meistertrunk" (Whit weekend, and selected other occasions).

This play by Adam Hörber, which is based on the famous story of the councillor who saved the town from destruction by winning a wager to down $3^{1}/_{4}$ litres of wine in a single draught, is performed in the Kaisersaal of the Rathaus.

Reichstadtfesttage (weekend in early September). During the "Free City Festival Days" groups re-create specific events and periods from Rothenburg's past in a variety of locations around the town. There are several markets, as well as street theatre, music and dancing. Performances of the Schäfertanz and "Der Meistertrunk" are both featured, and there is also a fireworks display.

Creglingen
Weinlaubenfest (weekend in late July) - wine festival.

Röttingen
Weintage (last weekend in May, or first weekend in June) - wine festival.
Festspiele (mid-July to mid-August) - open-air theatrical performances in the courtyard of Burg Brattenstein.
Gauvolksfest (late August) - summer fair.

Weikersheim
Maisingen (2nd Sunday in May) - festival of old customs.
Hauptstrassenfest (2nd Sunday in August) - summer fair.
Kärwe (1st weekend in September) - folk festival with costumed procession.

Bad Mergentheim
Stadtfest (weekend in late June) - summer fair.

Königshofen
Königshofer Messe (10 days from 3rd weekend in September) - smaller version of the famous Oktoberfest in Munich, with a market, a funfair and a giant beer tent.

Lauda
Taubergründer Weintage (1st weekend in June) - wine festival.

Tauberbischofsheim

Altstadtfest (weekend in early July) - summer fair.

Martini-Messe (weekend in mid-September) - autumn fair.

Würzburg

Würzburger Weindorf (late May and early June) - festival of Franconian food and wine, held in around 40 little huts set up in the city centre.

Bürgerspital Weinfest (late June) - festival of wines from the Bürgerspital's vineyards.

Hofgarten Weinfest (late June or early July) - festival of wines from the Hofkeller's vineyards.

Mozartfest (throughout June). In this celebration of the music of Mozart, some of the concerts are held outdoors in the Hofgarten, while others are performed indoors by candlelight in the Weisser Saal and Kaisersaal of the Residenz.

Kilianifest (two weeks in early July). For most of its duration, this festival honouring the Irish martyr St Kilian is a huge funfair. However, it begins on a Saturday afternoon with a costumed pageant of folklore groups through the city centre. The following morning, there is a solemn religious procession followed by high mass in the Dom.

Würzburger Weinfest - wine festival held in a huge tent.

Jazzfest (mid-November) - jazz festival.

Bachtage (late November and early December) - concerts of music by J.S. Bach.

CICERONE GUIDES

Cicerone publish a wide range of reliable guides to walking and climbing worldwide

FRANCE, BELGIUM & LUXEMBOURG
THE BRITTANY COASTAL PATH
CHAMONIX MONT BLANC - A Walking Guide
THE CORSICAN HIGH LEVEL ROUTE: GR20
FRENCH ROCK
THE PYRENEAN TRAIL: GR10
THE RLS (Stevenson) TRAIL
ROCK CLIMBS IN BELGIUM & LUXEMBOURG
ROCK CLIMBS IN THE VERDON
TOUR OF MONT BLANC
TOUR OF THE OISANS: GR54
TOUR OF THE QUEYRAS
TOUR OF THE VANOISE
WALKING IN THE ARDENNES
WALKING THE FRENCH ALPS: GR5
WALKING IN HAUTE SAVOIE
WALKING IN THE TARENTAISE & BEAUFORTAIN ALPS
WALKING THE FRENCH GORGES (Provence)
WALKS IN VOLCANO COUNTRY (Auvergne)
THE WAY OF ST JAMES: GR65

FRANCE / SPAIN
WALKS AND CLIMBS IN THE PYRENEES
ROCK CLIMBS IN THE PYRENEES

SPAIN & PORTUGAL
WALKING IN THE ALGARVE
ANDALUSIAN ROCK CLIMBS
BIRDWATCHING IN MALLORCA
COSTA BLANCA CLIMBS
MOUNTAIN WALKS ON THE COSTA BLANCA
ROCK CLIMBS IN MAJORCA, IBIZA & TENERIFE
WALKING IN MALLORCA
THE MOUNTAINS OF CENTRAL SPAIN
THROUGH THE SPANISH PYRENEES: GR11
WALKING IN THE SIERRA NEVADA
WALKS & CLIMBS IN THE PICOS DE EUROPA
THE WAY OF ST JAMES: SPAIN

SWITZERLAND including adjacent parts of France and Italy
THE ALPINE PASS ROUTE
THE BERNESE ALPS
CENTRAL SWITZERLAND
CHAMONIX TO ZERMATT The Walker's Haute Route
THE GRAND TOUR OF MONTE ROSA (inc Italy) 2 vols
WALKS IN THE ENGADINE
THE JURA - Walking the High Route and Winter Ski Traverses
WALKING IN TICINO
THE VALAIS - A Walking Guide

GERMANY / AUSTRIA / EASTERN & NORTHERN EUROPE
WALKING IN THE BAVARIAN ALPS
GERMANY'S ROMANTIC ROAD A guide for walkers and cyclists
HUT-TO-HUT IN THE STUBAI ALPS
THE HIGH TATRAS
KING LUDWIG WAY
KLETTERSTEIG - Scrambles
MOUNTAIN WALKING IN AUSTRIA
WALKING IN THE BLACK FOREST
WALKING IN THE HARZ MOUNTAINS
WALKING IN NORWAY
WALKING IN THE SALZKAMMERGUT

ITALY & SLOVENIA
ALTA VIA - High Level Walks in the Dolomites
THE CENTRAL APENNINES OF ITALY Walks, scrambles & Climbs
THE GRAND TOUR OF MONTE ROSA (inc Switzerland)
WALKS IN ITALY'S GRAN PARADISO
LONG DISTANCE WALKS IN THE GRAN PARADISO
ITALIAN ROCK - Rock Climbs in Northern Italy
VIA FERRATA - Scrambles in the Dolomites
WALKING IN THE DOLOMITES
WALKS IN THE JULIAN ALPS

MEDITERRANEAN COUNTRIES
THE ATLAS MOUNTAINS
CRETE: Off the beaten track
WALKING IN CYPRUS
THE MOUNTAINS OF GREECE
THE MOUNTAINS OF TURKEY
TREKS & CLIMBS IN WADI RUM, JORDAN
THE ALA DAG - Climbs & Treks (Turkey)

HIMALAYA & OTHER COUNTRIES
ANNAPURNA TREKKERS GUIDE
EVEREST - A TREKKER'S GUIDE
LANGTANG, GOSAINKUND & HELAMBU A Trekker's Guide
MOUNTAIN WALKING IN AFRICA 1: KENYA
OZ ROCK - A Rock Climber's guide to Australian Crags
ROCK CLIMBS IN HONG KONG
TREKKING IN THE CAUCAUSUS
ADVENTURE TREKS IN NEPAL
ADVENTURE TREKS - WESTERN NORTH AMERICA
CLASSIC TRAMPS IN NEW ZEALAND

GENERAL OUTDOOR BOOKS
THE ADVENTURE ALTERNATIVE
ENCYCLOPAEDIA OF MOUNTAINEERING
FAR HORIZONS - Adventure Travel for All!
THE TREKKER'S HANDBOOK
FIRST AID FOR HILLWALKERS
THE HILLWALKERS MANUAL
LIMESTONE -100 BEST CLIMBS IN BRITAIN
MOUNTAIN WEATHER
SNOW & ICE TECHNIQUES
ROPE TECHNIQUES IN MOUNTAINEERING

UK & IRELAND
Our list covers almost everywhere in the UK, with a great variety of books to suit all outdoor tastes

Ask for our catalogue which also shows our UK range of guidebooks to walking - short walks, family walks, long distance treks, scrambling, ice-climbing, rock climbing, and other adventurous pursuits. New titles are constantly added

Available from bookshops, outdoor equipment shops or direct (send for price list) from
CICERONE PRESS, 2 POLICE SQUARE, MILNTHORPE, CUMBRIA, LA7 7PY

PRINTED BY
CARNMOR PRINT & DESIGN, PRESTON, UK